# 1 Family and friends

## A Foundation exercises

### Vocabulary: Numbers 0–100

**1 Match the words with the numbers.**

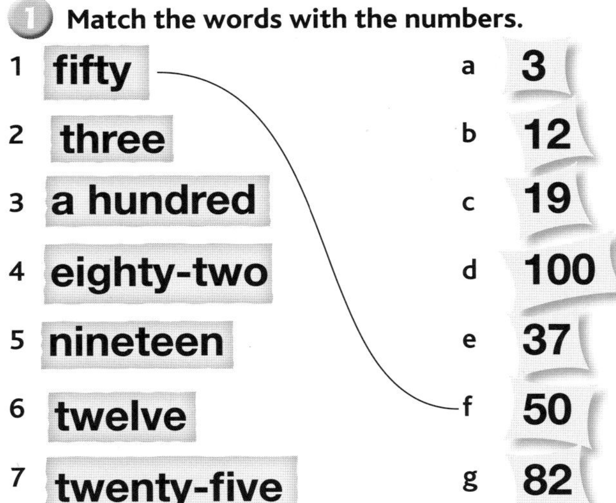
| 1 | fifty | a | 3 |
| 2 | three | b | 12 |
| 3 | a hundred | c | 19 |
| 4 | eighty-two | d | 100 |
| 5 | nineteen | e | 37 |
| 6 | twelve | f | 50 |
| 7 | twenty-five | g | 82 |
| 8 | thirty-seven | h | 25 |


### Grammar: *to be*

**2 Write the names.**

| Anna ~~Mark~~ Megan Will |
|---|

**3 Choose the correct words.**

1 I ('m) / *are* Will.
2 You *'m* / *'re* Mark.
3 My name *is* / *are* Anna.
4 *Am* / *Are* you new in this class?
5 How old *am* / *are* you?
6 Your name *is* / *are* Megan.
7 I*'m* / *are* new here.

**4 Complete the tables.**

| | |
|---|---|
| I [1] ...*'m*... | eleven. |
| You [2] ............ | |

| | |
|---|---|
| [3] ............ you eleven? | Yes, I [4] ............ . / No, I [5] ............ . |

| |
|---|
| What [6] ............ your name? |
| My name [7] ............ Mark. |

**5 Choose the correct answers.**

1 What's your name?
(a) I'm Joe. b I'm thirteen.
2 Are you new here?
a Yes, I am. b I'm Anna.
3 How old are you?
a No, I'm not. b I'm eleven.
4 What's your name?
a I'm ten years old. b My name's Will.
5 Are you Megan?
a Yes, I am. b Megan is my sister.
6 How old are you?
a No, I'm not. b I'm thirteen years old.
7 Are you at Newham High School?
a Yes, I am. b I'm Will.
8 Are you OK?
a I'm Megan. b I'm fine, thanks.

# A Activation exercises

## Vocabulary: Numbers 0–100

**1 Find and write the numbers.**

1 *64* ........ *sixty-four* ........

2 ........ ........

3 ........ ........

4 ........ ........

5 ........ ........

6 ........ ........

**2 Write the next number. Then write the numbers in words.**

1 5, 10, 15, 20, *25* *five, ten, fifteen,* ........

2 40, 50, 60, 70, ...... *forty, fifty,* ........

3 25, 50, 75, ...... *twenty-five,* ........

## Grammar: *to be*

**3 Match the questions with the answers.**

1 Are you at Newham High School?
2 Are you eleven?
3 Are you new in this class?
4 What's your name?
5 How old are you?
6 Are you Megan?

a No, I'm not. I'm twelve.
b My name's Darius.
c Yes, I am.
d Yes, I am. I'm in Class 1B.
e No, I'm not. I'm Anna.
f I'm sixteen.

**4 Find a photo or draw a picture of you. Then answer the questions.**

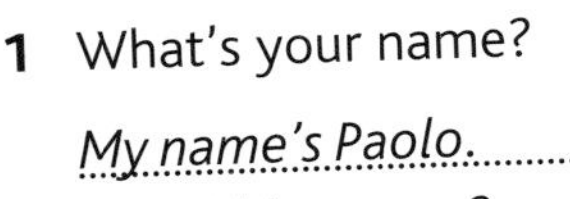

1 What's your name?

*My name's Paolo.* ........

2 How old are you?

*I'm twelve.* ........

1 What's your name?

........

2 How old are you?

........

## 5 Write the words in the correct order.

1 hello, | Megan | name's | my — *Hello, my name's Megan.*
2 are | you? | old | how — ..........
3 twelve | old | I'm | years — ..........
4 hi, | new | are | here? | you | Will! — ..........
5 name? | hello! | your | what's — ..........
6 is | sister | my | Anna — ..........

## English today

## 6 Complete the dialogue.

| Bye! fine Great! Hi OK problem ~~Sorry!~~ See you |
|---|

**Lee:** [1] *Sorry!*
**Mirka:** No [2] ..........!
**Lee:** Are you [3] ..........?
**Mirka:** I'm [4] .........., thanks.
**Lee:** [5] .......... Are you new in this class?
**Mirka:** Yes, I am!
**Lee:** What's your name?
**Mirka:** My name's Mirka.
**Lee:** [6] .........., Mirka! I'm Lee.
**Mirka:** Hello, Lee. [7] .......... soon!
**Lee:** Yes, OK. [8] ..........

## 7 Look at the table. Write two more dialogues.

| | Name | Age | New? |
|---|---|---|---|
| 1 | Harry | 12 | ✓ |
| 2 | Gemma | 11 | ✗ |
| 3 | Stephen | 13 | ✓ |

1 **A:** Hello! *What's your name?*
**B:** *I'm Harry.*
**A:** *How old are you, Harry?*
**B:** *I'm twelve.*
**A:** *Are you new here?*
**B:** *Yes, I am.*

2 **A:** Hi! *What's* ..........
**B:** .......... *Gemma.*
**A:** *How* ..........
**B:** *I'm* ..........
**A:** *Are* ..........
**B:** *No,* ..........

3 **A:** Hello! ..........
**B:** ..........
**A:** ..........
**B:** ..........
**A:** ..........
**B:** ..........

# A Extension exercises

## Vocabulary: Numbers 0–100

**1 Write the numbers in words.**

1 25 + 14 = 39 *twenty-five* + *fourteen* = *thirty-nine*

2 65 – 15 = 50 .................... – .................... = ....................

3 25 × 3 = 75 .................... × .................... = ....................

4 99 ÷ 33 = 3 .................... ÷ .................... = ....................

5 81 – 17 = 64 .................... – .................... = ....................

6 72 ÷ 9 = 8 .................... ÷ .................... = ....................

**2 Complete the crossword.**

1 100
2 81
3 38
4 13
5 24
6 75
7 59
8 62
9 46
10 93

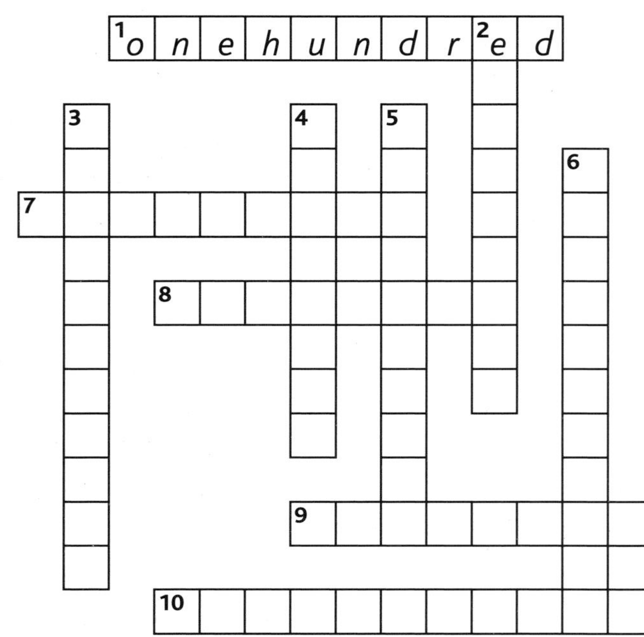


## Grammar: *to be*

**3 Write questions and answers.**

1 **A:** (you / Peter?) *Are you Peter?*
**B:** (✓) *Yes, I am.*

2 **A:** (how old / you?) ....................
**B:** (I / 15) ....................

3 **A:** (what / your name?) ....................
**B:** (I / Danny) ....................

4 **A:** (you / new here?) ....................
**B:** (✗) ....................

5 **A:** (you / Katie?) ....................
**B:** (✓) ....................

6 **A:** (what / your name?) ....................
**B:** (name / Yasmina) ....................

## About you

**4 Answer the questions about you.**

1 What's your name?

....................

2 Are you seventeen?

....................

3 How old are you?

....................

4 Are you new in this school?

....................

5 Are you new in this class?

....................

# B Foundation exercises

## Vocabulary: Formal greetings; The time

**1 Complete the greetings.**

1 G*o*od mor*n*ing!
2 Go.....d af.....ernoon!
3 Goo..... eve.....ing!

**2 Match the clocks with the times.**

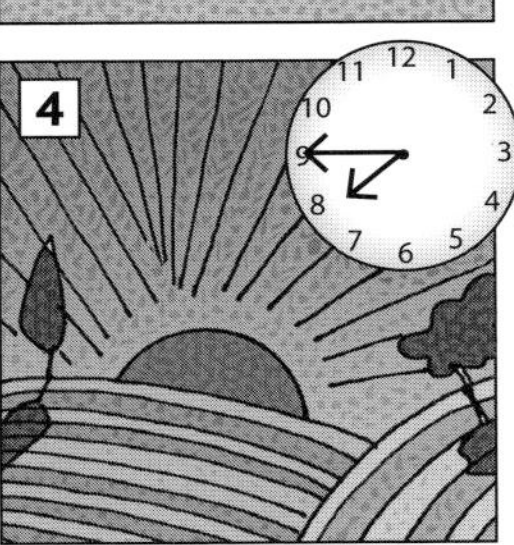

a half past two
b quarter past one
c quarter to eight
d six o'clock
e ten past eight
f twenty past seven

**3 Write the correct greetings for the times in Exercise 2.**

1 *Good morning!*
2 ..........
3 ..........
4 ..........
5 ..........
6 ..........

## Grammar: *to be; Who's ...?; his/her*

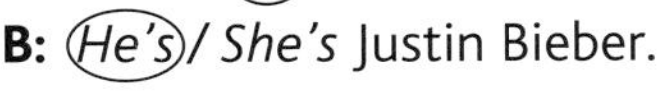

**4 Choose the correct words.**

1 **A:** Who's *he* / *she*?
**B:** *He's* / *She's* Justin Bieber.

2 **A:** Who's *he* / *she*?
**B:** *He's* / *She's* Lady Gaga.

3 **A:** Who's *he* / *she*?
**B:** *He's* / *She's* Johnny Depp.

4 **A:** Who's *he* / *she*?
**B:** *His* / *Her* name's Keira Knightley.

5 **A:** Who's *he* / *she*?
**B:** *He's* / *She's* Beyoncé.

6 **A:** Who's *he* / *she*?
**B:** *His* / *Her* name's Cristiano Ronaldo.

# B Activation exercises

## Vocabulary: Formal greetings; The time

**1 Write the letters in the correct order to make the greetings.**

1 doog teoonafrn *Good*..........................!
2 godo engevin ..............................!
3 oodg nimogrn ..............................!

**2 Find the correct stickers.**

1 It's seven o'clock.
2 It's twenty past four.
3 It's quarter to three.
4 It's quarter past eight.
5 It's twenty-five past two.
6 It's ten to eleven.

**3 [3 01] Listen and number the pictures. Match the times of the TV programmes with the clocks.**

a ........

b ........

c ........

d ...*1*...

e ........

f ........

## Grammar: *to be; Who's ...?; his/her*

**4 Complete the dialogues with *he*, *she*, *he's* or *she's*.**

1 A: Who's ...*he*...?
B: ...*He's*... Tom Cruise.
2 A: Who's ....................?
B: .................... Will Smith.
3 A: Who's ....................?
B: .................... Lady Gaga.
4 A: Who's ....................?
B: .................... Beyoncé.
5 A: Who's ....................?
B: .................... Justin Bieber.
6 A: Who's ....................?
B: .................... Jay-Z.

**5 Choose the correct words.**

1 She's Lady Gaga. *His* / (*Her*) hair's great!
2 That's Anna. Mark is *his* / *her* brother.
3 That's Mark. Anna is *his* / *her* sister.
4 He's Jay-Z. *His* / *Her* hair's cool.
5 That's Will. *His* / *Her* class is 1B.
6 She's Megan. Newham High is *his* / *her* school.

## English today

**6 Complete the dialogue.**

| ~~Come~~ | cool | It's time for | Wow! |
|---|---|---|---|

**Jodie:** Hi, James! 1 ......*Come*...... in.
**James:** Hi, Jodie.
**Jodie:** What time is it?
**James:** It's six o'clock.
**Jodie:** Great! 2 .............................. *Star World*.
**James:** 3 .............................. Look, it's Eminem!
He's 4 ..............................!
**Jodie:** Yes, he is!

**7 Complete the dialogue.**

| He's | he's | Her | she | She's | That's | ~~Who's~~ | Who's |
|---|---|---|---|---|---|---|---|

# Pop stars

*Bryan Lee with the stars*

**Bryan:** 1 ...*Who's*... that? Oh, 2 .................. Daniel Radcliffe!
And who's 3 ..................? Wow! 4 .................. Emma Watson!
She's cool. 5 .................. hair is great. Emma, hello!
**Emma:** Hello. Who are you?
**Bryan:** I'm Bryan Lee from *Pop Stars*.
**Emma:** Hi, Bryan. 6 .................. that?
**Bryan:** 7 .................. Eminem!
**Emma:** Wow! 8 .................. a great rapper! Bye, Bryan!

**8 Write about a pop star and find a photo. Use these ideas to help you.**

Write about:

- his/her name.
- his/her age.
- his/her job.
- his/her hair.

# Pop stars

..............................................................................................

..............................................................................................

..............................................................................................

..............................................................................................

..............................................................................................

..............................................................................................

..............................................................................................

..............................................................................................

# B Extension exercises

## Vocabulary: The time

**1** **Write the times.**

12:45

1 *quarter to one*

03:40

2 ....................

06:25

3 ....................

03:15

4 ....................

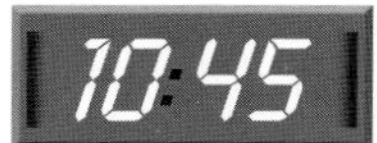


5 ....................

6 ....................

08:50

7 ....................

10:00

8 ....................

## Grammar: *to be; Who's ...?; his/her*

**2** **Look at the table. Write about Mark, Anna and Mrs Price.**

|  | 1 | 2 | 3 |
|---|---|---|---|
| **Name** | Mark | Anna | Gina |
| **Age** | 11 | 11 | 35 |
| **Family** | Anna, sister | Gina, mother | Mark, son |

1 *His name's Mark. He's eleven. Anna is his sister.*

....................

2 ....................

....................

3 ....................

....................

**3** **Write about Lady Loca. Add your own ideas: Is she cool? Is she great?**

Fact file

Name: Lady Loca

Age: 22

Job: Pop singer

**Who's that?**

*Her name's* ....................

....................

....................

....................

....................

## About you

**4** **Answer the questions.**

1 What's the time now?

....................

2 What's your favourite TV programme?

....................

3 What time's your favourite TV programme?

....................

4 What's your mum's name?

....................

5 How old is she?

....................

6 What's her favourite TV programme?

....................

7 What's your favourite star's name?

....................

8 How old is he/she?

....................

# C Foundation exercises

## Vocabulary: Days of the week; Family members

**1 Write the days of the week in the correct order.**

Friday ~~Monday~~ Saturday Sunday Thursday Tuesday Wednesday

**2 Complete the family words.**

1 gran*d*fat*h*er
2 gr....ndmo....her
3 f....ther
4 m....ther
5 b....other
6 sis....er

## Grammar: *to be*

**3 Complete the dialogues with *'s*, *is* or *isn't*.**

1 **A:** Who's Anna?
**B:** She *'s* my sister.
2 **A:** ........ she your aunt?
**B:** No, she ........ .
3 **A:** How old ........ your brother?
**B:** Sixteen.
4 **A:** ........ he your uncle?
**B:** No, he ........ .
5 **A:** ........ it your cat?
**B:** Yes, it ........ .

**4 Complete the dialogues.**

he He's is ~~isn't~~ isn't it she

1 **A:** Is she your cousin?
**B:** No, she *isn't*.
2 **A:** Is she your sister?
**B:** Yes, ........ is.
3 **A:** How old ........ she?
**B:** She's eight years old.
4 **A:** Is ........ your grandfather?
**B:** Yes, he is.
5 **A:** How old is he?
**B:** ........ sixty-seven.
6 **A:** Is he your brother?
**B:** No, he ........ . He's my cousin.
7 **A:** Is it your cat?
**B:** No, ........ isn't.

# C Activation exercises

## Vocabulary: Days of the week; Family members

**1 Find and write five days of the week. Then write the two missing days.**

~~MON~~ ~~DAY~~ DAY FRI TUES THURS DAY DAY SUN DAY

1 ......*Monday*......
2 ..............................
3 ..............................
4 ..............................
5 ..............................

The missing days:

6 ..............................
7 ..............................

**2 Complete Lamar's family tree.**

| aunt | brother | cousin | father (dad) | ~~grandfather~~ | grandmother | mother (mum) | sister | uncle |
|---|---|---|---|---|---|---|---|---|

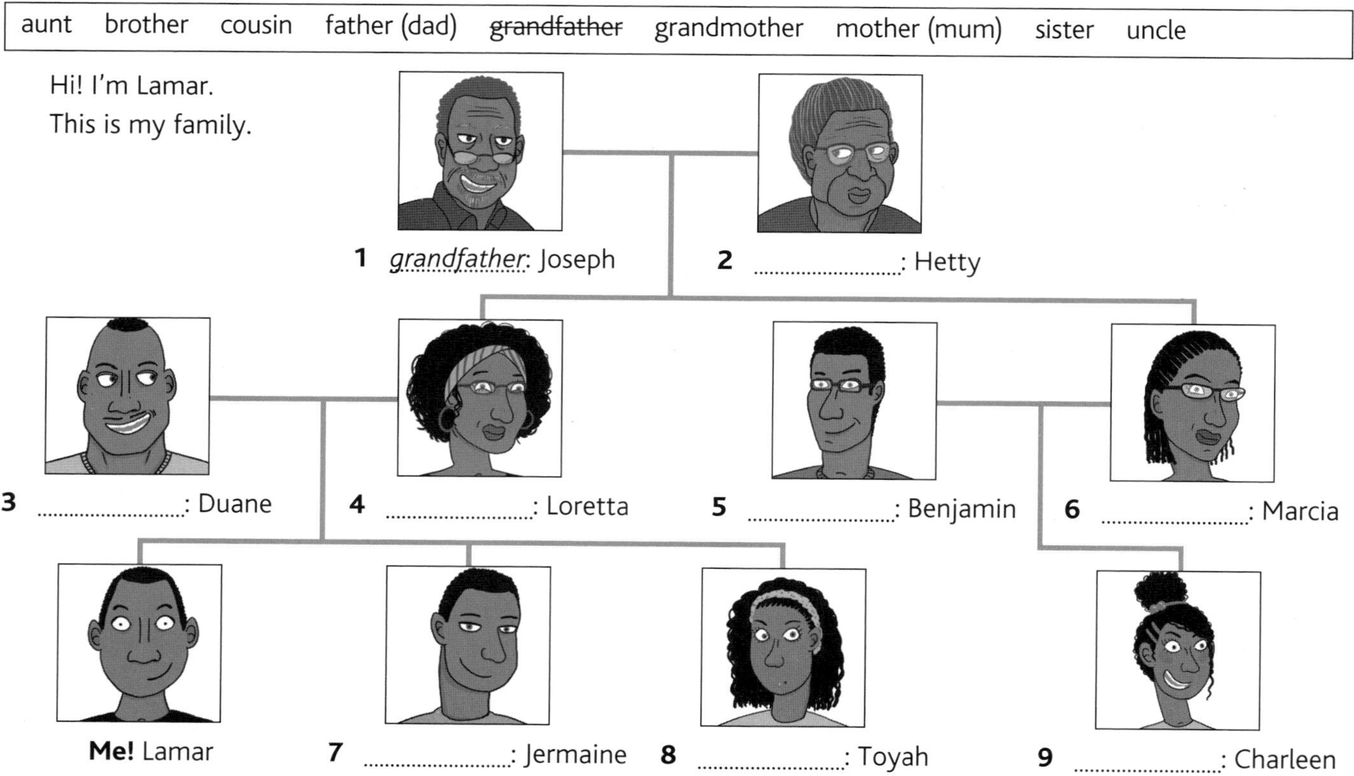


## Grammar: *to be*

**3 Complete the table.**

| Verb *to be* | | |
|---|---|---|
| + | - | ? |
| I [1] ...*'m*.../am | I'm not/[2] .................. | Am I? |
| You're /[3] .................. | You aren't/are not | [4] .................. you? |
| He<br>She [5] ................../[6] ..................<br>It | He<br>She [7] ................../is not<br>It | he?<br>[8] .................. she?<br>it? |

## 4 Choose the correct answers.

1 Who ...... she?
   a 's  b it
2 How old ...... he?
   a it  b is
3 He .......... my brother.
   a isn't  b not
4 ...... it your cat?
   a 's  b Is
5 She ...... my friend.
   a he  b 's
6 Who ...... he?
   a 's  b he's

## 5 Match the questions with the answers.

1 How old is she?
2 Is she your grandmother?
3 Is that your T-shirt?
4 Is he your brother?
5 How old is he?
6 How old is your cat?

a It's four years old.
b Yes, he is.
c She's twelve.
d He's fourteen.
e No, she isn't.
f Yes, it is.

## 6 Look at Lamar's family tree in Exercise 2. Ask Lamar questions about his family.

1 (Loretta) she / mother?
   *Is she your mother?*
2 (Hetty) how old / she?
   ..........
3 (Duane) he / brother?
   ..........
4 (Benjamin) he / uncle?
   ..........
5 (Marcia) she / aunt?
   ..........
6 (Toyah) she / cousin?
   ..........
7 (Toyah) how old / she?
   ..........

## 7 Write Lamar's answers to the questions in Exercise 6.

1 *Yes, she is.*
2 (70) ..........
3 ..........
4 ..........
5 ..........
6 ..........
7 (15) ..........

## About you

## 8 Answer the questions about you.

1 Is Anna your sister?
   *No, she isn't.*
2 Is *Pop World* your favourite TV programme?
   ..........
3 Is your grandmother fifty years old?
   ..........
4 How old is she?
   ..........
5 Is your father twenty-one years old?
   ..........
6 Is Lady Gaga your favourite pop singer?
   ..........
7 Is Saturday your favourite day?
   ..........

## English today

## 9 Complete the dialogue.

| Call | OK | tomeet | ~~Welcome~~ | Yum! |
|---|---|---|---|---|

**Robert:** Hello, Mia. Are you Mark's friend? [1] *Welcome* to the barbecue.
**Mia:** Thank you, Robert. Yes, I am! Nice [2] .......... you.
**Robert:** [3] .......... me Rob.
**Mia:** [4] .........., Rob.
**Robert:** It's burgers today. Is that OK?
**Mia:** Oh yes! [5] ..........

# C Extension exercises

## Vocabulary: Days of the week; Family members

**1 Write the days of the week in the correct order.**

| | |
|---|---|
| 1 ...*Monday*... | 4 ............ |
| 2 ............ | 5 ............ |
| 3 ............ | 6 ............ |
| | 7 ............ |

**2 Write the words in the correct group.**

| |
|---|
| ~~aunt~~ brother cat cousin father grandfather grandmother mother sister uncle |

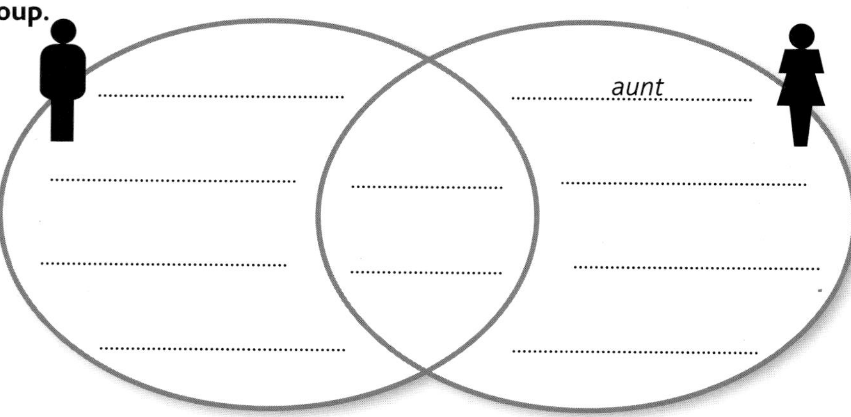


## Grammar: *to be*

**3 Write the family words and the names and answer the questions about your family.**

Your ............: ............

1 Is she twenty-three? *No, she isn't.*

2 How old is she? ............

Your ............: ............

3 Is she old? ............

4 How old is she? ............

Your ............: ............

5 Is he ninety-eight? ............

6 How old is he? ............

Your ............: ............

7 Is he twenty? ............

8 How old is he? ............

## About you

**4 Find photos or draw pictures of two family members and complete the fact file. Then write sentences.**

| fact file | | |
|---|---|---|
| Name | | |
| Age | | |
| Favourite TV programme | | |

*This is Jo. She's my mum. She's thirty years old. Her ...*

1 ............

............

2 ............

............

# Welcome to the English club! Saturday at ten o'clock

## Speaking: Ask for personal information

**1 Match the questions with the answers. There are two extra answers.**

1 What's your first name? — c
2 What's your phone number?
3 What's your surname?
4 Can you spell that?
5 What's your address?

a D-E-C-K-H-A-M.
b I'm thirty-two.
c It's David.
d 01132 584 310.
e I'm fine, thanks.
f It's Deckham.
g 26, Dearside Road.

### Your turn

**2 Write the questions from Exercise 1 in the dialogue. Then answer the questions about you.**

**Teacher:** [1] (first name) *What's your first name?* ..........
**You:** ..........
**Teacher:** [2] (surname) ..........
**You:** ..........
**Teacher:** [3] (spell) ..........
**You:** ..........
**Teacher:** [4] (address) ..........
**You:** ..........
**Teacher:** [5] (phone) ..........
**You:** ..........

## Writing: Complete a membership card

**3 Find and correct the mistakes in the membership card. Write capital letters in the correct places.**

english club
Name: angela robinson
Age: 12
Address: 14 main road, newtown
Phone number: 594763
english club is at ten o'clock on saturdays

### Your turn

**4 Find and correct the mistakes in the membership card. Write capital letters in the correct places. Then complete the card with your information. Add a photo.**

english club
Name
Age
Address
Phone number
english club is at ten o'clock on saturdays

# Check

**1 Choose the correct answers to complete the dialogue.**

TALKING WITH THE STARS
## Lady Loca
BY WILL DIAMOND

LL: Hello! Welcome to my house! [1] ....... Will?
WD: Yes. Good afternoon, Miss Loca. Nice to meet you.
LL: Call me Lucy.
WD: [2] ....... that in the photo? Is [3] ....... your mum?
LL: No, she [4] .......! She's my favourite singer!
WD: Silly me! What's [5] ....... name?
LL: Her name's Dannii Minogue.
WD: [6] ....... she Kylie Minogue's sister?
LL: Yes, she [7] ........ Oh, is it Saturday today?
WD: Yes, [8] ....... is.
LL: And what time is it?
WD: [9] ....... half past five.
LL: Great! It's time for my favourite TV programme, *Talking With The Stars*!

Kylie Minogue
Dannii Minogue

1 (a) Are you b He's
2 a It's b Who's
3 a he b she
4 a is b isn't
5 a his b her
6 a Is b Her
7 a is b isn't
8 a he b it
9 a She's b It's

**Score:** ........ /8

**2 Which word is different? Choose.**

| | | | |
|---|---|---|---|
| 1 | three | five | (you) |
| 2 | Monday | Mark | Sunday |
| 3 | mum | friend | dad |
| 4 | twenty | Wow! | forty |
| 5 | good | past | o'clock |
| 6 | what | how | time |
| 7 | he | Jay-Z | she |
| 8 | cousin | morning | evening |

**Score:** ........ /7

**Colour one ring on Lenny's tail for each correct answer.**

My score is ..................!

# 2 People and places

## A Foundation exercises

### Vocabulary: Countries and nationalities

**1 Complete the countries.**

1 the *U* SA
2 B.....a.....il
3 .....rg.....ntina
4 C.....in.....
5 A.....st.....alia

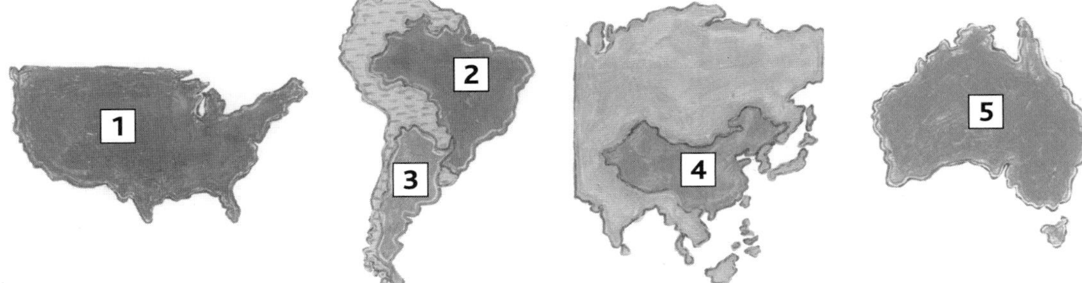


**2 Write the nationalities.**

| ~~British~~ | Greek | Italian | Polish | Portuguese | Spanish | Turkish |
|---|---|---|---|---|---|---|

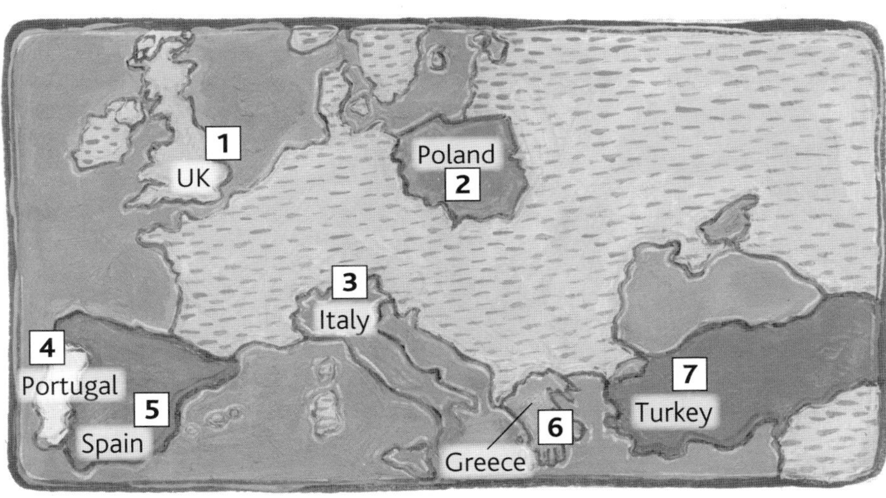


1 ........*British*........
2 ..............................
3 ..............................
4 ..............................
5 ..............................
6 ..............................
7 ..............................

### Grammar: to be; our/their

**3 Choose the correct words.**

1 We *is* / *'re* Spanish. (*'re* circled)
2 We *not* / *aren't* Italian.
3 They *isn't* / *aren't* from the UK.
4 They *am* / *'re* Greek.
5 They *am* / *'re* from Poland.
6 We *is* / *'re* Italian.
7 We *am not* / *aren't* from the USA.
8 We *am* / *'re* Portuguese.

**4 Match the questions with the answers.**

1 Are they Italian? — d
2 Are you and your family Greek?
3 Where are they from?
4 Are you and your friend twelve years old?
5 Are they British?
6 Are their names Kelly and Maisie?

a No, we aren't. We're Spanish.
b No, we aren't. We're eleven years old.
c No, their names are Katie and Macey.
d Yes, they are.
e No, they aren't. They're American.
f They're from Argentina.

# A Activation exercises

## Vocabulary: Countries and nationalities

**1 Complete the table.**

| Country | Nationality |
|---|---|
| Turkey | 1 *Turkish* |
| 2 ........................ | Argentinian |
| Brazil | 3 ........................ |
| Greece | 4 ........................ |
| Italy | 5 ........................ |
| 6 ........................ | Australian |
| China | 7 ........................ |
| 8 ........................ | Spanish |

## Grammar: *to be; our/their*

**2 Complete the sentences with *are*, *'re* or *aren't*.**

1 They (✗) *aren't* from Portugal.
2 We (✓) .................. from the UK.
3 We (✗) .................. American.
4 Our names (✓) .................. Stefan and Petra.
5 We (✓) .................. Canadian.
6 Their names (✓) .................. Iza and Michal.
7 They (✓) .................. from Poland.
8 They (✗) .................. new in this class.

**3 Write questions and answers. Use *we*, *you* and *they*.**

1 you / from Italy?
A: *Are you from Italy?*
B: (✗) *No, we aren't.*
2 they / Argentinian?
A: ..................................................
B: (✓) ..................................................
3 you and your brother / Polish?
A: ..................................................
B: (✓) ..................................................
4 you and your friends / from the UK?
A: ..................................................
B: (✗) ..................................................
5 they / Portuguese?
A: ..................................................
B: (✗) ..................................................

**4 Answer the questions.**

1 A: Are they from Portugal?
B: *No, they aren't. They're from the UK.*

2 A: Are they from the USA?
B: ..................................................

3 A: Are they Spanish?
B: ..................................................

4 A: Are they Argentinian?
B: ..................................................

**5 Complete the sentences with *our* or *their*.**

1 They're Canadian. *Their* names are Lee and Eve.
2 We're British. .............. names are Joe and Freya.
3 We're Italian. .............. names are Dino and Chiara.
4 They're Australian. .............. names are Mia and Zac.
5 They're Spanish. .............. names are Maria and Juan.
6 We're Polish. .............. names are Marcin and Aldona.

**6 Write questions.**

1 where / they / from?

A: *Where are they from?*

B: They're from Italy.

2 they / Spanish?

A: ..................................................

B: Yes, they are.

3 they / from Canada?

A: ..................................................

B: No, they aren't.

4 you and your friend / students?

A: ..................................................

B: Yes, we are.

5 what / their names?

A: ..................................................

B: Their names are George and Sonia.

## English today

**7 Complete the speech bubbles.**

| Excuse me. | Go and ask them. | You're joking! |
|---|---|---|

..................................................

1

..................................................

2

..................................................

3

**8 Read the text and answer the questions.**

### N-Dubz

Tulisa, Dappy and Fazer are pop singers in the UK. Dappy and Tulisa are brother and sister. They're from London but their dad is Greek. Tulisa is twenty-four years old. She's on TV and she is very famous in the UK. Fazer is their friend. He's twenty-five.

1 Are they students?

*No, they aren't. They're pop singers.*

2 Where are Tulisa and Dappy from?

..................................................

3 Is their dad from the UK?

..................................................

4 How old is Tulisa?

..................................................

5 Is Tulisa famous in the UK?

..................................................

6 Are Dappy and Fazer brothers?

..................................................

7 Who's Fazer?

..................................................

8 How old is Fazer?

..................................................

**9 Write questions and answers about your favourite pop singer or singers. Use Exercise 8 to help you.**

1 ..................................................

..................................................

2 ..................................................

..................................................

3 ..................................................

..................................................

4 ..................................................

..................................................

# A Extension exercises

## Vocabulary: Countries and nationalities

**1 Complete the nationalities.**

| -an | -ese | -ian | -ish | -k |
|---|---|---|---|---|

1 Brit*ish*
2 Gree.........
3 Turk.........
4 Portugu.........
5 Argentin.........
6 Brazil.........
7 Pol.........
8 Span.........
9 Canad.........
10 Chin.........
11 Americ.........
12 Austral.........

**2 Write the countries from Exercise 1.**

1 ............*the UK*............
2 ........................
3 ........................
4 ........................
5 ........................
6 ........................
7 ........................
8 ........................
9 ........................
10 ........................
11 ........................
12 ........................

## Grammar: to be; our/their

**3 Write questions and answers.**

1 you and your friend / from the UK?
A: *Are you and your friend from the UK?*
B: (✗ / USA) *No, we aren't. We're from the USA.*

2 you and your friend / from Spain?
A: ........................
B: (✗ / Italy) ........................

3 they / from Poland?
A: ........................
B: (✓) ........................

4 you and your friend / from Brazil?
A: ........................
B: (✓) ........................

5 they / from Turkey?
A: ........................
B: (✗ / Argentina) ........................

## About you

**4 Answer the questions about you. Find a photo or draw a picture of your family or friends.**

1 Are you and your friends British?
........................
2 Are your friends Chinese?
........................
3 Where are you and your friends from?
........................
4 How old are your friends?
........................
5 Where are your grandfather and grandmother from?
........................
6 What are their names?
........................
7 How old are they?
........................
8 Where are your father and mother from?
........................
9 What are their names?
........................
10 How old are they?
........................

# B Foundation exercises



## Vocabulary: Everyday objects

**1 Write the words.**

| apple | cake | ice cream | MP3 player | orange | sandwich | strawberry | ~~umbrella~~ |
|---|---|---|---|---|---|---|---|

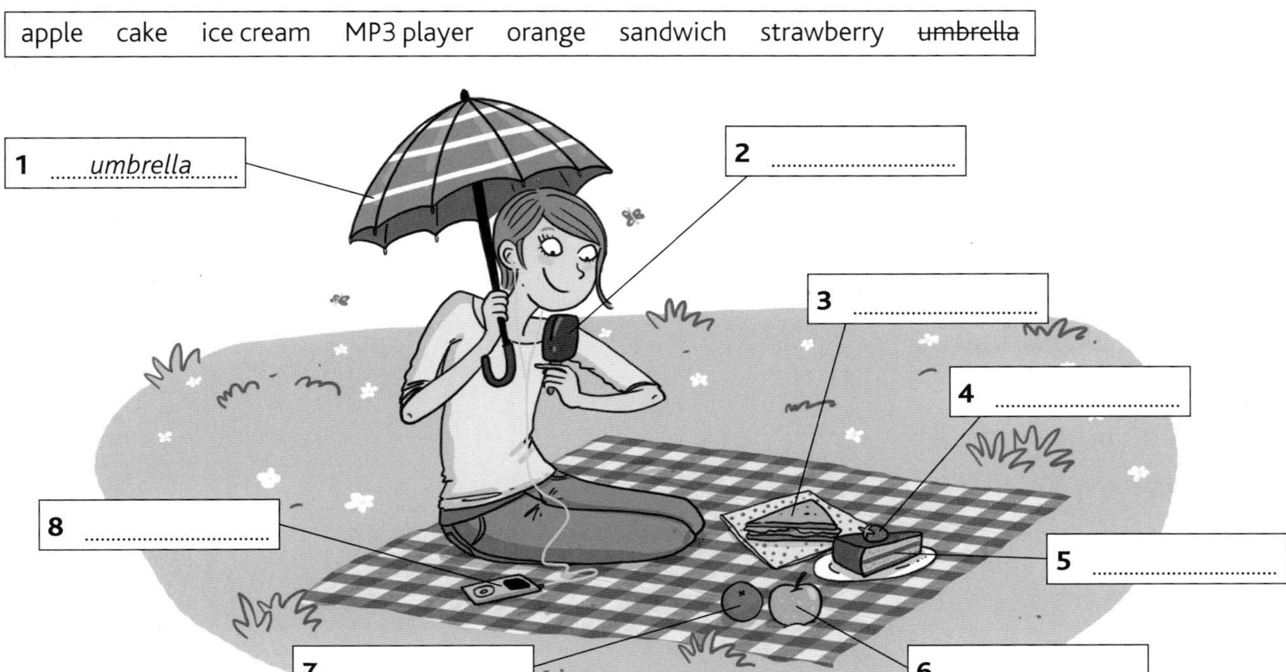


**2 Complete the words.**

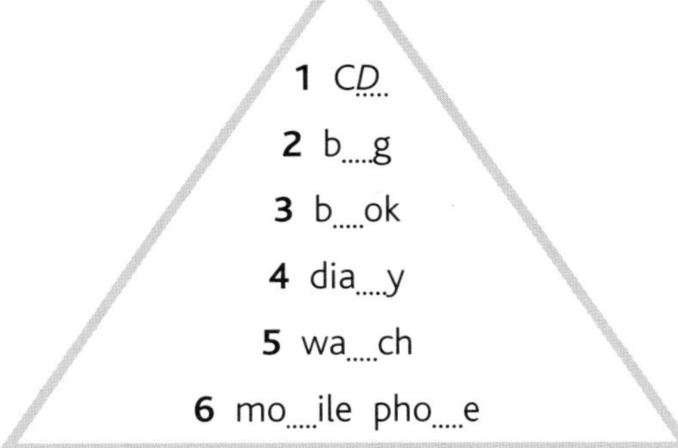

1 C*D*
2 b....g
3 b....ok
4 dia....y
5 wa....ch
6 mo....ile pho....e


## Grammar: *a/an*; Plural nouns; *this, that, these, those*

**3 Complete the words with *-s*, *-es* or *-ies*.**

| | One | Two or more |
|---|---|---|
| 1 | diary | diar*ies* |
| 2 | orange | orange........ |
| 3 | sandwich | sandwich........ |
| 4 | watch | watch........ |
| 5 | strawberry | strawberr........ |
| 6 | mobile phone | mobile phone........ |

**4 Complete the table with *this*, *that*, *these* or *those*.**

**A:** What's [1] ......................?
**B:** It's a cake.

**A:** What's [2] ......................?
**B:** It's an umbrella.

**A:** What are [3] ......................?
**B:** They're sandwiches.

**A:** What are [4] ......................?
**B:** They're mobile phones.

# B Activation exercises

## Vocabulary: Everyday objects

**1** 3 02 **What's in Nina's bag? Listen and tick (✓).**

| | | | | | | | |
|---|---|---|---|---|---|---|---|
| 1 book | ✓ | 5 mobile phone | ☐ | 9 orange | ☐ |
| 2 MP3 player | ☐ | 6 diary | ☐ | 10 apple | ☐ |
| 3 CD | ☐ | 7 ice cream | ☐ | 11 watch | ☐ |
| 4 cake | ☐ | 8 umbrella | ☐ | 12 sandwich | ☐ |

**2** **Which word is different? Choose.**

1 umbrella ice cream (bag)
2 apple mobile phone orange
3 MP3 player CD umbrella
4 strawberry diary ice cream
5 diary book cake
6 orange watch sandwich

## Grammar: *a/an*; Plural nouns; *this, that, these, those*

**3** **Write *a* or *an* and the word. Then write the plural.**

| | *A/An ...* | Plural |
|---|---|---|
| 1 | *a strawberry* | *strawberries* |
| 2 | ........................ | ........................ |
| 3 | ........................ | ........................ |
| 4 | ........................ | ........................ |
| 5 | ........................ | ........................ |
| 6 | ........................ | ........................ |
| 7 | ........................ | ........................ |
| 8 | ........................ | ........................ |

### 4 Find the correct stickers.

1 **A:** What are these?
**B:** They're CDs.

2 **A:** What are those?
**B:** They're books.

3 **A:** What are these?
**B:** They're ice creams.

4 **A:** What's that?
**B:** It's an umbrella.

5 **A:** What's this?
**B:** It's a book.

6 **A:** What are these?
**B:** They're umbrellas.

### 5 Choose the correct words.

1 **A:** What's (*that*) / *those*? Is it a book?
**B:** No, (*it's*) / *they're* a diary.
2 **A:** What *is* / *are* these?
**B:** *It's* / *They're* our family photos.
3 **A:** What are *that* / *those*?
**B:** *It's* / *They're* sandwiches. Yum!
4 **A:** What's *this* / *those*?
**B:** *It's* / *They're* a watch. What's the time?
5 **A:** What's *that* / *these*?
**B:** *It's* / *They're* my mobile phone.

## English today

### 6 Complete the dialogue.

| Brilliant! | ~~Here!~~ | Oh no! | Really? | why |
|---|---|---|---|---|

**Sara:** This is for you, Robbie. [1] *Here!*
**Robbie:** Thanks, Sara! Is it a present?
**Sara:** No, it isn't. It's a cake.
**Robbie:** [2] .................. Great! Is it a strawberry and ice cream cake?
**Sara:** Yes, it is!
**Robbie:** [3] .................. My favourite!
**Sara:** And this is your present.
**Robbie:** Wow! It's a CD – the Black Eyed Peas! Thanks! But ... [4] ..................?
**Sarah:** Because it's your birthday, silly!
**Robbie:** Thanks, but ... er ... my birthday is on Friday.
**Sara:** [5] ..................

### 7 Read Freya's blog and answer the questions.

Today's my birthday. I'm twelve years old. My presents are:
- a mobile phone (Mum and Dad) AND a bag! Wow!
- a T-shirt (my brother, Ben)
- a diary (my sister, Sadie)

Today is my party. My cake is an ice cream cake with strawberries and oranges. Yum! My favourite cake!

These are my friends at my birthday party:
♥ Jodie ♥ Michael ♥ Harry ♥ Olivia

Bye!
Freya

1 How old is Freya today?
*She's twelve years old.*
2 What are her presents from her mum and dad?
..................
3 Is Ben her brother?
..................
4 Is Sadie her cousin?
..................
5 What's her favourite cake?
..................
6 Are Michael and Olivia her friends?
..................

### 8 Write a blog about your birthday party. Use Exercise 7 to help you.

# B Extension exercises

## Vocabulary: Everyday objects

**1 What's this? Find the words and write sentences. There are six extra words.**

| | | | | | |
|---|---|---|---|---|---|
| apple | ~~bag~~ | book | cake | CD | diary |
| ice cream | mobile phone | MP3 player | orange | | |
| sandwich | strawberry | umbrella | watch | | |

1 gba *It's a bag.*
2 anoreg ..........
3 3PM yeplar ..........
4 ndchsawi ..........
5 plape ..........
6 DC ..........
7 cie eacrm ..........
8 okbo ..........

## About you

**2 What's in your school bag? Look at the words in Exercise 1 to help you.**

..........
..........
..........
..........
..........
..........

## Grammar: *a/an*; Plural nouns; *this, that, these, those*

**3 Choose and write the correct questions.**

1 *What's this? / What are these?*
A: *What are these?* B: They're ice creams.
2 *What's this? / What are those?*
A: .......... B: They're our bags.
3 *What's this? / What are these?*
A: .......... B: It's my umbrella.
4 *What's that? / What are those?*
A: .......... B: It's a mobile phone.
5 *What's this? / What are these?*
A: .......... B: They're cakes.
6 *What's that? / What are those?*
A: .......... B: They're apples.

**4 Write questions and answers.**

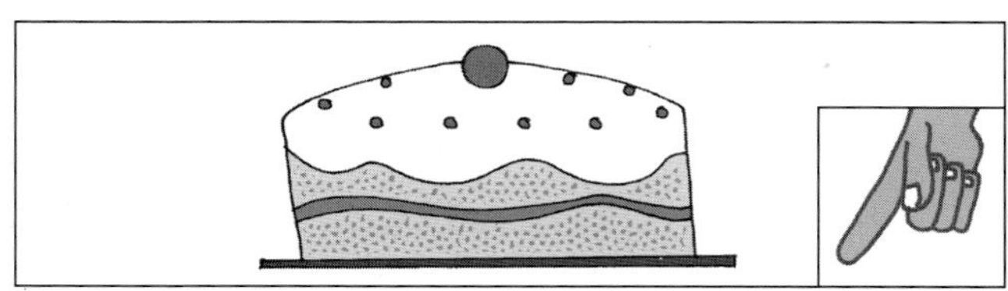

1 A: *What's this?*
B: *It's a cake.*

2 A: ..........
B: ..........

3 A: ..........
B: ..........

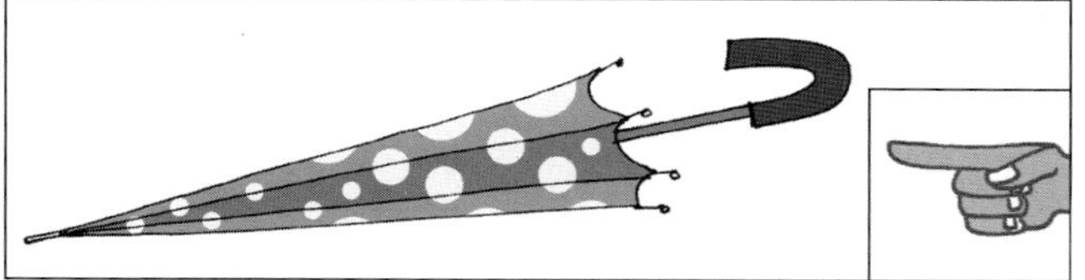

4 A: ..........
B: ..........

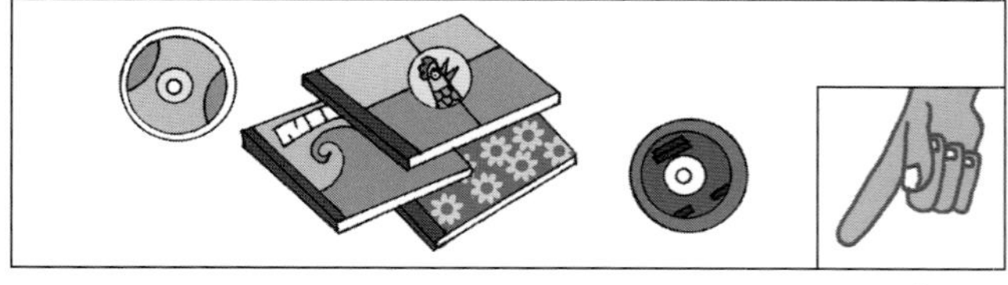

5 A: ..........
B: ..........

6 A: ..........
B: ..........

## Speaking: Talk about music

**1 Complete the dialogue.**

awesome ~~favourite singer~~ from the UK
Is she Listen to this

**Amy:** Who's your [1] *favourite singer* ?
**Lisa:** My favourite singer's Katy Perry.
**Amy:** [2] .......... CD. It's Adele. She's [3] ..........!
**Lisa:** [4] .......... American?
**Amy:** No, she isn't. She's [5] ...........
**Lisa:** Wow! She's brilliant!

Adele

### Your turn

**2 Complete the dialogue between you and your friend about your favourite singers. Use Exercise 1 to help you.**

**Your friend:** Who's [1] *your favourite singer* ?
**You:** My [2] ...........
**Your friend:** Listen to [3] ...........
It's [4] ...........
[5] .......... awesome!
**You:** Is [6] ..........?
**Your friend:** [7] ..........!

## Writing: Write about your favourite music programme

**3 Find and correct the mistakes in the blog. Write capital letters for the countries and nationalities.**

My favourite TV programme is ~~britain's~~ *Britain's* *Got Talent*. It's famous in the uk. The *Got Talent* programmes are famous in argentina, australia, canada, china, greece, italy, poland, portugal, spain and the usa, too. A great american singer from *america's Got Talent* is Jackie Evancho. She's twelve years old and she's an opera singer. She's awesome! Listen to her CD!

**4 Write about your favourite music programme on TV. Use Exercise 3 to help you.**

..........
..........
..........
..........
..........
..........
..........
..........

# Check

**1** **Read the text and choose the correct words.**

**Beth:** We're twelve years old today! It's our birthday!
**Sam:** My presents are a bag and two CDs (Pixie Lott and Coldplay).
**Beth:** And my presents are an MP3 player and two *Harry Potter* books!
**Beth and Sam:** Our party's at five o'clock. Our friends at the party are Cristina and Jorge (they're from Argentina), Anna and Petros (they're Greek), and Tim and Tara (they're British). Our birthday cake is our favourite – ice cream with strawberries. Yum!

Beth Sam

Hi, Beth! Happy Birthday!
Hello, Sam! Happy Birthday!


1 Beth and Sam are *sisters* / *aunts*.
2 Beth and Sam are *eleven* / *twelve* years old today.
3 Today is *Tuesday* / *their birthday*.
4 (Sam) Her presents are two CDs and *a bag* / *a diary*.
5 (Beth) Her presents are books and *a mobile phone* / *an MP3 player*.
6 Cristina and Jorge are *Brazilian* / *Argentinian*.
7 Anna and Petros are from *the UK* / *Greece*.
8 Tim and Tara are from *the UK* / *the USA*.
9 Their favourite cake is ice cream with *oranges* / *strawberries*.

**Score:** ........ **/8**

**2** **Complete the sentences.**

| are | from | Our | that | They're | ~~We're~~ | What | Who's |
|---|---|---|---|---|---|---|---|

1 *We're* Italian.
2 Where are they ..................?
3 Hi! .................. names are Kasia and Marcin.
4 'What's ..................?' 'It's your present.'
5 .................. Polish.
6 'What .................. those?' 'They're CDs.'
7 .................. your favourite singer?
8 .................. are their names?

**Score:** ........ **/7**

**Colour one ring on Lenny's tail for each correct answer.**

My score is ..................!

# 3 House and home

## A Foundation exercises

### Vocabulary: The house

**1 Complete the house words.**

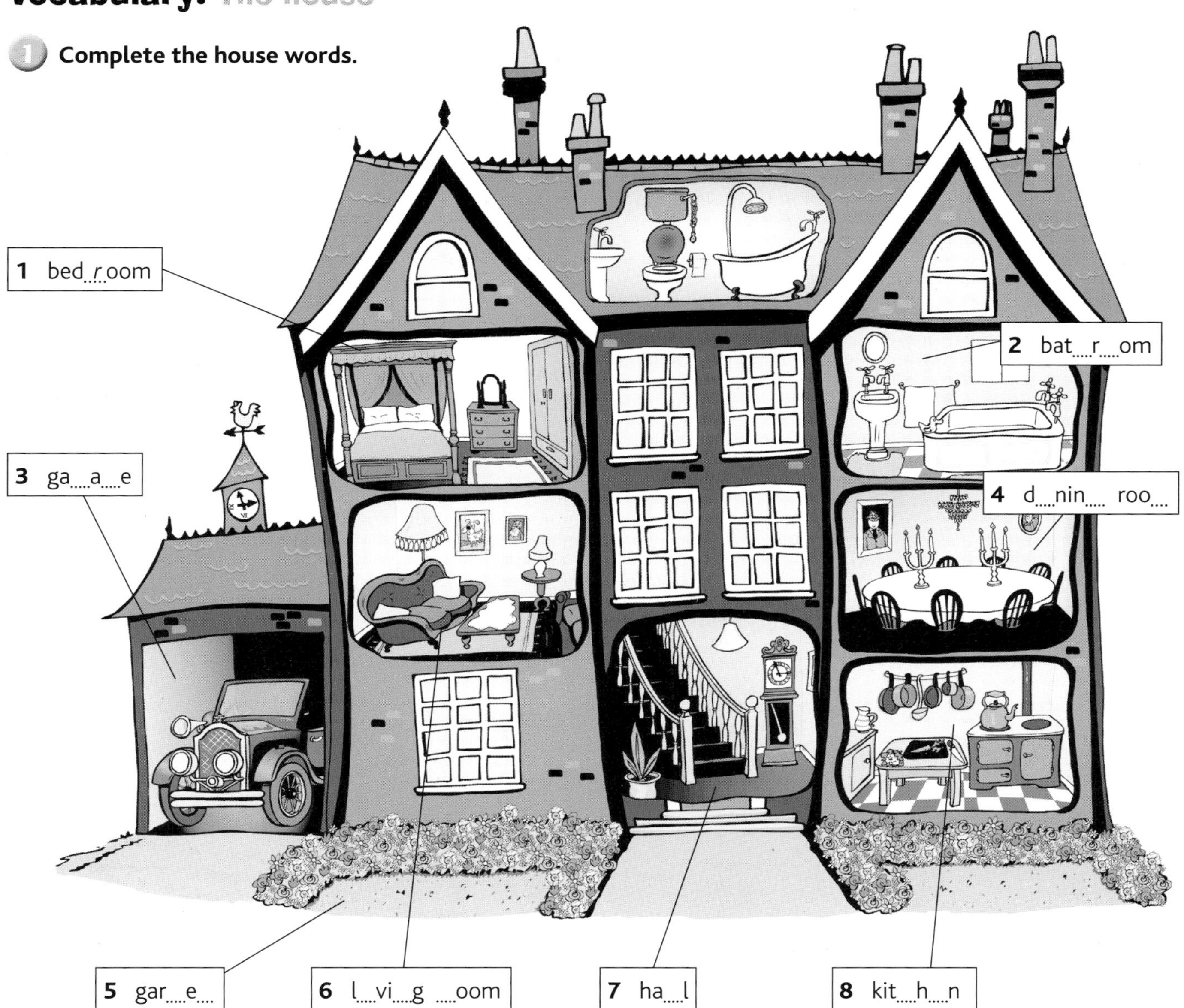


### Grammar: *there is/are*

**2 Choose the correct words.**

1 There *is* / *are* (circled) three bedrooms.
2 There *is* / *are* a dining room.
3 There *is* / *are* a garden.
4 There *is* / *are* two bathrooms.
5 There *is* / *are* six rooms.
6 There *is* / *are* a garage.
7 There *is* / *are* two cars in the garage.
8 There *is* / *are* a kitchen.

**3 Complete the dialogues.**

| Are | are | are | aren't | Is | isn't | ~~there~~ | there |
|---|---|---|---|---|---|---|---|

1 **A:** Are *there* four rooms?
**B:** No, there .................... .
2 **A:** .................... there a hall?
**B:** No, there .................... .
3 **A:** .................... there three bedrooms?
**B:** Yes, .................... are.
4 **A:** How many bathrooms .................... there?
**B:** There .................... two.

# A Activation exercises

## Vocabulary: The house

**1 Write the letters in the correct order to make the house words.**

1 rdngae ............*garden*............
2 vilngi orom ..........................
3 thombaro ..........................
4 raegag ..........................
5 tcenkih ..........................
6 nignid oorm ..........................
7 alhl ..........................
8 drmbeoo ..........................

**2 Write the house words.**

1 .......................... ☐
2 .......................... ☐
3 .......................... ☐
4 .......................... ☐
5 .......................... ☐
6 .......................... ☐
7 .......................... ☐
8 ............*garden*............ ✓

**3 3/03 Look at Exercise 2. Listen and tick (✓) the words you hear.**

**4 Complete the table.**

| + | - | ? | |
|---|---|---|---|
| *There* [1] *'s* /There is | There [2] .............. | Is there ...? | Yes, there [3] ..............<br>No, there isn't. |
| There [4] .............. | [5] .............. aren't | Are there ...? | Yes, there are.<br>No, there [6] ............... |

## Grammar: *there is/are*

**5 Choose the correct words.**

**Anna:** My favourite house is my cousin's house. There [1] (*is*) / *are* a big garden.
**Will:** [2] *Is* / *Are* there lots of flowers in the garden?
**Anna:** Yes, and there [3] *is* / *are* lots of rooms in the house.
**Will:** How many rooms [4] *is* / *are* there?
**Anna:** There [5] *is* / *are* nine! No, ten! Oh, I'm not sure!
**Will:** [6] *Is* / *Are* there a computer?
**Anna:** Yes, there [7] *is* / *are*. And there [8] *is* / *are* a big TV.
**Will:** Cool!

**6 Read and answer *True* (*T*) or *False* (*F*).**

## Stars and their houses

Hi! I'm Simon Cowell. My favourite house is in Los Angeles in the USA. There are six bedrooms and six bathrooms. There are MP3 players in the bedrooms for my friends. There's a big living room but there isn't a dining room in the house. There are three garages and a big garden. My house is cool!

1. His favourite house is in the UK. F
2. There are eight bedrooms and bathrooms. ☐
3. There are CDs in the bedrooms. ☐
4. There are MP3 players in the bathrooms. ☐
5. There's a living room in the house. ☐
6. There's a big garden. ☐

**7 Write questions about Simon's house.**

1. how many / bedrooms / there?
   *How many bedrooms are there?*
2. how many / bathrooms / there?
   ............................................
3. there / MP3 players / in the bedrooms?
   ............................................
4. there / a mobile phone / in the living room?
   ............................................
5. there / a dining room / in the house?
   ............................................
6. how many / garages / there?
   ............................................

## English today

**8 Complete the dialogue. There is one extra phrase.**

| Come in! | it's nice | lovely to see you | nice surprise |
|---|---|---|---|

**Harry:** Here's a cake for Grandma. It's a surprise! It's her birthday today.
**Alice:** Great!
**Gran:** Hi, kids! How [1] ..............................!
[2] ..............................
**Harry:** Happy birthday, Grandma! Here's a cake!
**Gran:** Yum! What a [3] ..............................! Thanks, kids!

# A Extension exercises

## Vocabulary: The house

**1 Make seven house words. Use some letters more than once.**

| bath | gar | room | bed |
|---|---|---|---|
| en | ing | kitch | age |
| liv | gard | din | |

1 bathroom
2 ..........
3 ..........
4 ..........
5 ..........
6 ..........
7 ..........

Write one more room:

..........

## Grammar: *there is/are*

**2 Match the pictures with the texts. There is one extra picture.**

a

b

c

d

1 This house is in Australia. There's one big room. The kitchen and the living room are in this room! There's a small bathroom and a bedroom, too. ......

2 This is a British house. There's one bedroom and a living room. There's a small kitchen and bathroom but there isn't a dining room. There are lots of flowers in the garden. ......

3 There's one room in this American house – it's a living room. There isn't a bedroom, there isn't a bathroom and there isn't a kitchen. It's in a tree! ......

**3 Write about the extra picture in Exercise 2. Use the notes to help you.**

✓ eleven rooms
✓ big living room
✓ dining room
✓ four bedrooms
✓ four bathrooms
✓ kitchen downstairs

*This house is in Canada. There are eleven rooms. Upstairs there are* ..........

..........

..........

..........

..........

## About you

**4 Answer the questions about your home.**

1 Are there two bathrooms in your house/flat?
*Yes, there are./No, there aren't.*
2 Are there three bedrooms?
..........
3 How many rooms are there?
..........
4 Is there a TV in the bedroom?
..........
5 Are there lots of books?
..........
6 Is there a garden?
..........

# B Foundation exercises

## Vocabulary: Colours; Common possessions

**1 Complete the possessions.**

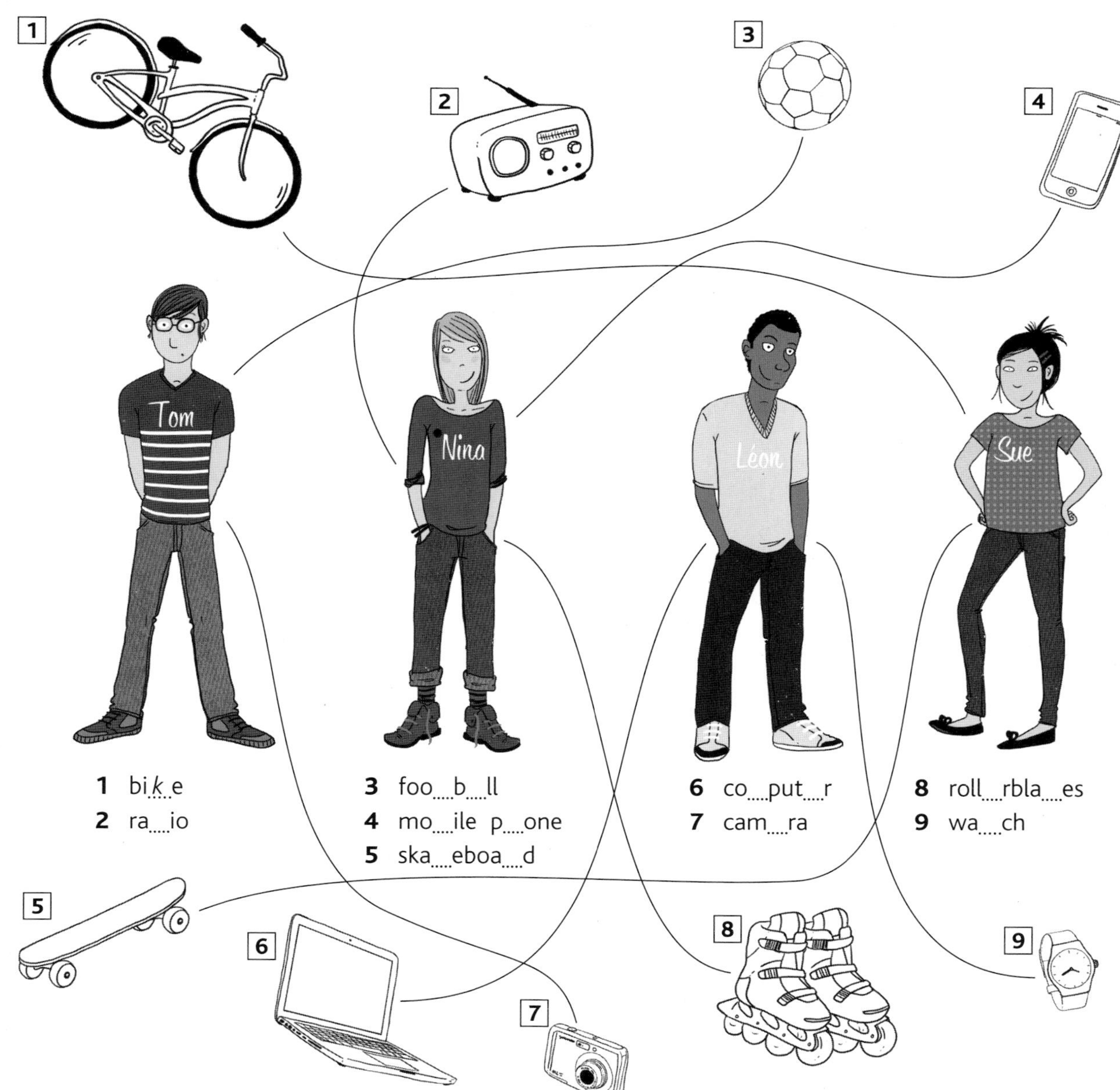


**2 Read and colour the possessions in Exercise 1.**

1 The bike is blue.
2 The camera is green.
3 The football is black and white.
4 The computer is grey.
5 The mobile phone is purple.
6 The radio is brown.
7 The rollerblades are yellow.
8 The skateboard is orange.
9 The watch is red.

## Grammar: *Whose … ?*; Possessive *'s*

**3 Whose is it? Follow the lines in Exercise 1 and complete the answers.**

1 (bike) It's *Sue's*.
2 (computer) It's ..........................
3 (skateboard) It's ..........................
4 (camera) It's ..........................
5 (radio) It's ..........................
6 (football) It's ..........................

# B Activation exercises

## Vocabulary: Colours; Common possessions

**1 Put the letters in the correct order and write the colours in the table.**

1 dre
2 ebul
3 llwyoe
4 rpepul
5 engre
6 yger
7 acblk
8 aneorg
9 owbrn
10 itweh

| | | | | | | | | | |
|---|---|---|---|---|---|---|---|---|---|
| 1 | *red* | 3 | ..... | 5 | ..... | 7 | ..... | 9 | ..... |
| 2 | ..... | 4 | ..... | 6 | ..... | 8 | ..... | 10 | ..... |

**2 Look at the numbers in Exercise 1 and colour the possessions.**

**3 Look at Exercise 2 and write the possessions.**

~~bike~~ camera computer football games console mobile phone radio rollerblades skateboard watch

1 *bike*
2 .....
3 .....
4 .....
5 .....
6 .....
7 .....
8 .....
9 .....
10 .....

## Grammar: *Whose ... ?*; Possessive *'s*

**4 Whose are they? Look at Exercise 2 and write sentences.**

1 Antonio: 1, 3

*It's Antonio's bike.*

*They're Antonio's rollerblades.*

2 my sister: 5, 6

.....

.....

3 Donna: 2, 4

.....

.....

4 Enrique: 7, 9

.....

.....

5 my parents: 8, 10

.....

.....

## 5 Write questions and answers.

1 Katy Perry

A: *Whose umbrella is it?*

B: *It's Katy Perry's umbrella.*

2 Lady Gaga

A: ..........

B: ..........

3 Justin Bieber

A: ..........

B: ..........

4 Daniel Radcliffe

A: ..........

B: ..........

5 Kristen Stewart

A: ..........

B: ..........

6 Will Smith

A: ..........

B: ..........

## About you

## 6 Answer the questions about things in your home.

1 Is there a camera in your house/flat?

*Yes, there is./No, there isn't.*

(Yes?) Whose camera is it?

*It's my dad's camera./It's my camera.*

2 Is there a computer in your living room?

..........

(Yes?) Whose computer is it?

..........

3 Is there an MP3 player in your bedroom?

..........

(Yes?) Whose MP3 player is it?

..........

4 Are there books in the dining room?

..........

(Yes?) Whose books are they?

..........

5 Is there a radio in the kitchen?

..........

(Yes?) Whose radio is it?

..........

6 Is there a bike in the house?

..........

(Yes?) Whose bike is it?

..........

## English today

## 7 Complete the dialogue. There is one extra phrase.

| Are you sure? | Let's see! |
|---|---|
| What else is there? | Whose is it? |

**Mark:** Look at this book, Anna! It's very old!
**Anna:** It isn't a book. It's a diary!
**Mark:** [1] ..........
**Anna:** Yes, I'm sure. Look. There's a name ...
**Mark:** [2] ..........
Yes, the name is Julia! And there's a *D* and an *I* and ...
**Anna:** [3] ..........
**Mark:** There's an *A* and ... is it an *R*?
**Anna:** Yes, it is. It's *JULIA'S DIARY*!

# B Extension exercises

## Vocabulary: Colours; Common possessions

**1 Write the letters in the correct order to make the possessions and colours. Then write the words in the correct columns.**

1 dorai *radio*
2 egyr ..................
3 onbrw ..................
4 nereg ..................
5 iekb ..................
6 aergno ..................
7 blfolota ..................
8 acemar ..................

| Possessions | Colours |
|---|---|
| *radio* | |
| | |
| | |
| | |

## Grammar: *Whose ... ?*; Possessive *'s*

**2 Follow the lines and write sentences.**

| | | | |
|---|---|---|---|
| 1 | Andy | skateboard | yellow |
| 2 | Peter | camera | white |
| 3 | Freya | watch | black |
| 4 | Lucy | mobile phone | purple |
| 5 | Dan | rollerblades | blue |
| 6 | Sasha | bike | red |

1 *Andy's watch is blue.*
2 ..................
3 ..................
4 ..................
5 ..................
6 ..................

**3 Write two possessions for each person. Then write sentences.**

| You | Your friend |
|---|---|
| *computer* | |
| | |

| Your mum or dad | Your cousin |
|---|---|
| | |
| | |

1 *It's my computer. It's white and grey.*
..................
2 ..................
..................
3 ..................
..................
4 ..................
..................

### About you

**4 Answer the questions about your school bag.**

1 What colour is your school bag?
*It's* ..................
2 What's in your school bag?
*There are four books. They're red and green and blue. There's an apple. It's red and green.*
..................
..................
..................

# C Foundation exercises

## Vocabulary: House and furniture

**1 Match the words with the pictures.**

a chair .......
b window .......
c bookcase .......
d cupboard .......
e wardrobe *1*
f TV (television) .......

**2 Complete the crossword.**

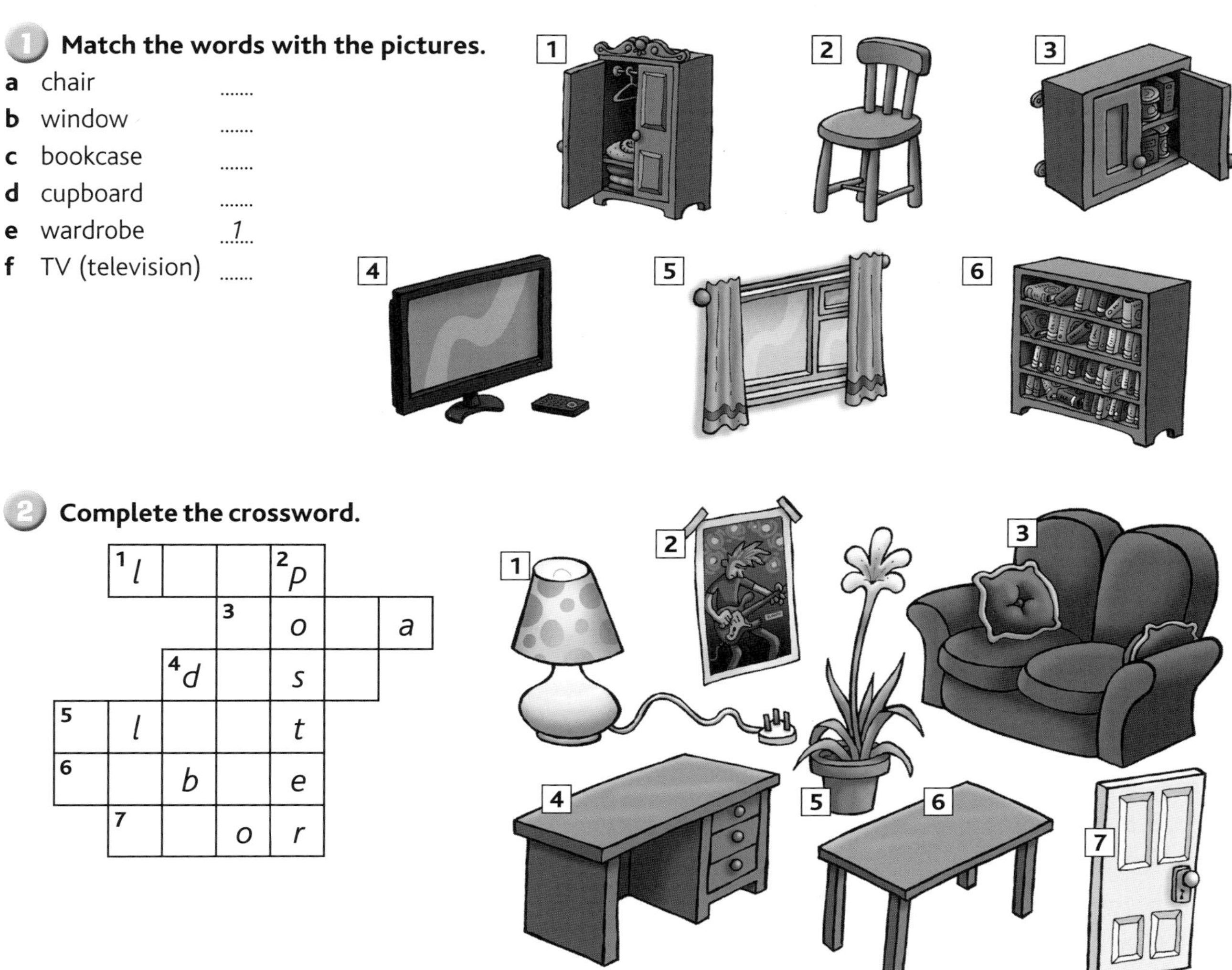


| | | | | | | |
|---|---|---|---|---|---|---|
| | 1 *l* | | | 2 *p* | | |
| | | | 3 | *o* | | *a* |
| | | 4 *d* | | *s* | | |
| 5 | *l* | | | *t* | | |
| 6 | | *b* | | *e* | | |
| | 7 | | *o* | *r* | | |

## Grammar: Prepositions

**3 Write the prepositions.**

| behind ~~in~~ in front of next to on under |
|---|

1 ..........*in*.......... the box

2 .................................. the box

3 .................................. the box

4 .................................. the box

5 .................................. the box

6 .................................. the box

# C Activation exercises

## Vocabulary: House and furniture

**1 Find thirteen house and furniture words.**

| T | E | L | E | V | I | S | I | O | N | C | N | T |
|---|---|---|---|---|---|---|---|---|---|---|---|---|
| A | D | F | W | B | K | T | L | Q | Z | J | W | B |
| B | O | O | K | C | A | S | E | R | W | P | I | D |
| L | S | Y | E | U | W | L | V | I | A | E | N | C |
| E | J | P | M | P | O | S | T | E | R | T | D | V |
| F | I | K | L | B | A | P | J | Y | D | O | O | R |
| B | O | L | F | O | X | D | G | N | R | Q | W | Y |
| J | U | S | L | A | M | P | K | W | O | D | H | S |
| W | O | R | H | R | J | L | H | Q | B | G | J | Q |
| P | N | F | P | D | H | A | S | D | E | S | K | I |
| T | S | A | L | B | G | N | Y | H | T | O | N | D |
| E | K | K | T | R | J | T | N | T | J | F | Q | E |
| R | X | O | I | P | S | E | P | C | H | A | I | R |

**2 Answer the questions.**

**In your classroom**

1 Is there a cupboard?

*Yes, there is./No, there isn't.*

2 (Yes?) What colour is the cupboard?

..................................................

3 How many chairs are there?

..................................................

4 What colour are the desks?

..................................................

5 How many windows are there?

..................................................

6 Is there a bookcase?

..................................................

**In your living room**

7 Is there a sofa?

..................................................

8 Is there a TV?

..................................................

9 Is there a wardrobe?

..................................................

10 How many lamps are there?

..................................................

## Grammar: Prepositions

**3 Find the correct stickers.**

1 The poster is under the desk.

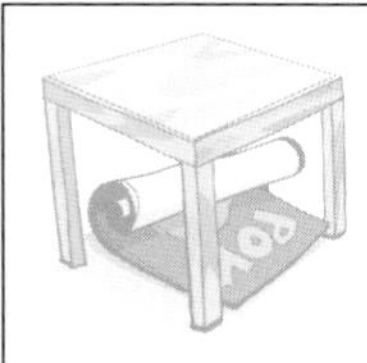

2 The lamp is behind the window.

3 The chair is on the sofa.

4 The plant is in the wardrobe.

5 The chair is in front of the sofa.

6 The lamp is next to the window.

**4 Write sentences.**

1 TV / in / living room

*The TV is in the living room.*

2 lamp / behind / sofa

..................................................

3 cupboard / next to / bookcase

..................................................

4 table / under / window

..................................................

5 plant / on / desk

..................................................

6 computer / in front of / plant

..................................................

## 5 Complete the dialogue.

*Sherlock Holmes and Dr Watson are in a big room.*

**S. Holmes:** Where's the sofa?
**Dr Watson:** (table) [1] *It's next to the table.* ..........
**S. Holmes:** Where are the chairs?
**Dr Watson:** (window) [2] *They're* ..........
**S. Holmes:** Where's the small lamp?
**Dr Watson:** (small table) [3] ..........
**S. Holmes:** Where's the big lamp?
**Dr Watson:** (sofa) [4] ..........
**S. Holmes:** Where's the plant?
**Dr Watson:** (big lamp) [5] ..........

## 6 Read Emily's blog and answer the questions.

# My blog:
## My dream bedroom

This is my dream bedroom. There's a big bed in my room and there are two chairs next to the window – one chair for me and one for my school bag! There's a bookcase next to the door and a computer on the desk. There are plants with red and white flowers on the bookcase and on the desk. And there's a sofa (MY sofa!) in front of a big TV. The sofa is my favourite thing! It's cool!

Emily

1 Is there a big bed in the room?
*Yes, there is.* ..........
2 Where are the chairs?
*They're* ..........
3 Is there a bookcase?
..........
4 Where's the computer?
..........
5 What are there on the desk?
..........
6 Where's the sofa?
..........
7 What's Emily's favourite thing?
..........

## 7 Write about your dream bedroom. Use the words in the box and Exercise 6 to help you.

| behind | in | in front of | next to |
|---|---|---|---|
| on | there's | there are | under |

# My blog:
## My dream bedroom

This is my dream bedroom. *There's a* ..........

..........

..........

..........

# C Extension exercises

## Vocabulary: House and furniture

**1** **Write the words.**

## Grammar: Prepositions

**2** **Look at the word pictures and complete the sentences. Then draw your own word picture and write a sentence.**

1 CHAIRWARDROBE

2 P L A N T TV

3 CUPBOARD SOFA

4 LIVING ROOM LAMP

5

1 The chair ........ *is next to the wardrobe* ........ .

2 The plant ................................................ .

The TV ................................................ .

3 The sofa ................................................ .

The cupboard ................................................ .

4 The lamp ................................................ .

5 ................................................ .

**3** **Write about your grandparents' house or your aunt and uncle's house. Use these questions to help you.**

**The house**

- How many rooms are there?
- What are the rooms?
- Is there a garden?

**The living room**

- What is/are there in the living room?
- What colour are they?
- How many windows are there?

My ............................ house

................................................................

................................................................

................................................................

................................................................

................................................................

# Communication



## Speaking: Show someone your home

**1** **Choose the correct answers.**

*Anna and Megan are in Megan's bedroom.*

**1** **Anna:** Hi, Megan.
**Megan:** **a** Goodbye, Anna!
(**b**) Hello, Anna!
**c** Cool, Anna!

**2** **Anna:** There isn't a bed!
**Megan:** **a** Yes, there is.
**b** Is it a bed?
**c** No, it isn't.

**3** **Anna:** Where is it?
**Megan:** **a** It's my sofa. Look!
**b** It's your sofa. Look!
**c** It's in the sofa! Look!

**4** **Anna:** Is that your computer?
**Megan:** **a** No, it's my mum's.
**b** No, there isn't.
**c** No, I'm not.

### Your turn

**2** **Complete the dialogue.**

| ~~Come in!~~ great colour nice really cool this is my |
|---|

**Anna:** Hi, Megan! 1 *Come in*!
**Megan:** Hi, Anna! Your room's very 2 .................................
And the wardrobe is a 3 .................................
**Anna:** Thanks! Purple is my favourite colour.
**Megan:** But ... where's the bed?
**Anna:** It's in the sofa! Look, 4 ................................. sofa bed!
**Megan:** That's 5 .................................!

## Writing: Describe your room

**3** **Choose the correct answers for 1–6 in Anna's email.**

**To:** kellyjones@meandmymail.com

**Subject:** A .................................................................................

B ....................... Kelly,

This 1 ..... a photo of my bedroom. It's cool! My bed is a big sofa bed. It's 2 ..... and purple. Purple is my favourite colour. 3 ..... a small wardrobe, two purple chairs and a desk. The computer is 4 ..... my desk. There 5 ..... a TV but there
6 ..... lots of books in the bookcase.

Tell me about your room!

C .......................,

Anna

| | | | | | |
|---|---|---|---|---|---|
| **1** **a** | am | (**b**) | is | **c** | are |
| **2** **a** | Polish | **b** | small | **c** | blue |
| **3** **a** | There's | **b** | There are | **c** | There |
| **4** **a** | on | **b** | in front of | **c** | behind |
| **5** **a** | am not | **b** | isn't | **c** | aren't |
| **6** **a** | am | **b** | is | **c** | are |

**4** **Choose the best title and write it in A in Anna's email.**

**1** Our living room
**2** My bedroom
**3** My mum's room

**5** **Complete the starting and ending phrases. Then write them in B and C in Anna's email.**

**1** D.... ....r (your friend's name),
**2** L.... ....e, (your name)

# Check

**1 Complete the text.**

| bathrooms | garage | in | in front of | ~~is~~ | many | their | there | white |
|---|---|---|---|---|---|---|---|---|

## A cool house

This [1] ..........*is*.......... Carleen and Ronald and this is [2] .................... house. It's really cool! It's in Pennsylvania, [3] .................... the USA. It's brown and [4] ..................... It isn't very big.

There are plants [5] .................... the house. How [6] .................... rooms are [7] .................... in the house? There are three bedrooms and two [8] ..................... There's a kitchen and a living room. But there isn't a dining room and there isn't a [9] .....................

Score: ........ /8

**2 Write the words in the correct columns.**

| ~~cupboard~~ | grey | hall | kitchen | my rollerblades | orange | wardrobe | Will's bike |
|---|---|---|---|---|---|---|---|

| Colours | Furniture | Possessions | Rooms |
|---|---|---|---|
| .................... | .....*cupboard*..... | .................... | .................... |
| .................... | .................... | .................... | .................... |

Score: ........ /7

**Colour one ring on Lenny's tail for each correct answer.**

My score is ..........!

# 4 Me and my things

## A Foundation exercises

### Vocabulary: Clothes

**1 Write the words.**

| boots | coat | ~~hat~~ | jacket | jeans | skirt | trainers | trousers | T-shirt |
|---|---|---|---|---|---|---|---|---|

**2 Complete the clothes words.**

1 short s  2 d...ess  3 shir...  4 j...mper  5 sh...es  6 c...p

### Grammar: *have got*

**3 Choose the correct words.**

1 (✓) *We've got* / *We haven't got* an MP3 player.
2 (✓) *I've got* / *I haven't got* a coat.
3 (✗) *I've got* / *I haven't got* any jeans.
4 (✗) *We've got* / *We haven't got* a towel.
5 (✓) *We've got* / *We haven't got* a camera.
6 (✓) *I've got* / *I haven't got* a white shirt.

**4 Complete the dialogues with *have* or *haven't*.**

1 A: *Have* you got a book?
B: Yes, I *have*.
2 A: ............ you got any dresses?
B: Yes, I ............ .
3 A: ............ you got any white shoes?
B: No, we ............ .
4 A: ............ you got a coat?
B: No, I ............ .

# A Activation exercises

## Vocabulary: Clothes

**1 Complete the crossword.**

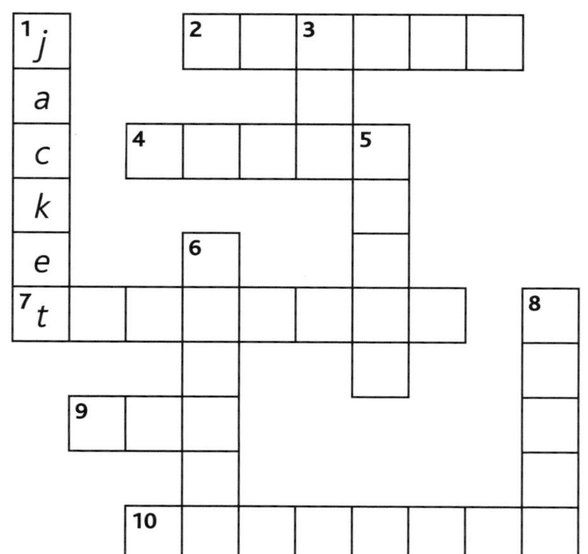

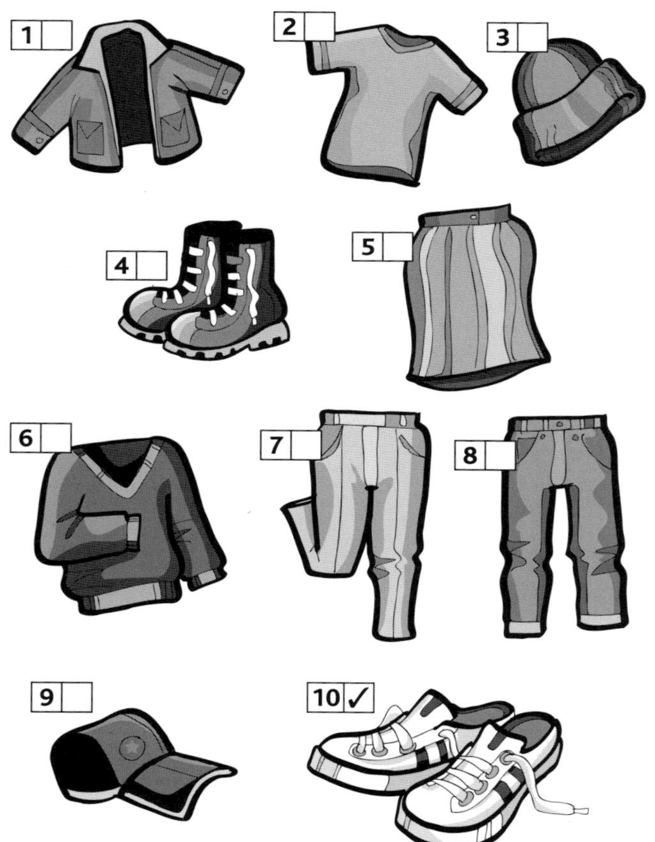

**2 3 04 Look at the pictures in Exercise 1. Listen and tick (✓) the words you hear.**

**3 Complete the clothes words. Then say the sentence five times, quickly.**

I've got a [1] sh*i* *r* t, some [2] sh..... es and some [3] ..... .....orts, a [4] c.....p, a [5] h.....t and a [6] j..... .....per.

## Grammar: *have got*

**4 Write negative sentences. Use *a* or *any*.**

1 I've got a jacket.
*I haven't got a jacket.*
2 We've got some CDs.
..........
3 We've got a new camera.
..........
4 I've got some black jeans.
..........
5 I've got a red coat.
..........
6 I've got some black shoes.
..........
7 We've got a new MP3 player.
..........

**5 Write questions.**

1 you / a blue jumper?
*Have you got a blue jumper?*
2 we / any sandwiches?
..........
3 you / an MP3 player?
..........
4 you / a big school bag?
..........
5 we / any football shirts?
..........
6 we / any white trainers?
..........
7 you / a red pen?
..........

**6** **Match the pictures with the texts. There is one extra picture.**

a

b

c

d

1 Hi! I've got an old white T-shirt and an old jacket but I've got a new hat and a new bag! ......

2 Hello! I'm Marvin and these are my friends. We've got some new T-shirts. There's a cool picture on the T-shirts. ......

3 I'm with my friends and we're at my birthday party. I've got some great presents! My friends and I have got new dresses. ......

## About you

**7** **Answer the questions about you.**

1 Have you got any trainers?
*Yes, I have./No, I haven't.*

2 Have you and your family got a TV?
..............................

3 Have you and your friend got any books?
..............................

4 Have you got a camera?
..............................

5 Have you got any white jeans?
..............................

6 Have you got any sandwiches in your bag?
..............................

## English today

**8** **Complete the dialogue.**

| Don't worry. | ~~Sorry I'm late.~~ |
|---|---|
| Wait a minute. | What's the matter? |

**Anna:** Hi, Mark. [1] *Sorry I'm late.* Are you ready?
**Mark:** Er ... no! [2] ..............................
**Anna:** [3] ..............................
**Mark:** I haven't got my books for school.
**Anna:** Where are they?
**Mark:** I'm not sure.
**Anna:** [4] .............................. They're behind the door. Look!
**Mark:** Oh! OK, now I'm ready! Let's go!

**9** **Write sentences.**

1 we / (✗) a TV / (✓) a radio
*We haven't got a TV but we've got a radio.*

2 I / (✗) any CDs / (✓) an MP3 player
..............................

3 I / (✗) any trainers / (✓) some shoes
..............................

4 we / (✗) a car / (✓) bikes
..............................

5 I / (✗) a coat / (✓) a jacket
..............................

6 we / (✗) a computer / (✓) a mobile phone
..............................

# A Extension exercises

## Vocabulary: Clothes

**1 Write the clothes words in the correct place.**

| boots | cap | coat | dress | hat | jacket | jeans | jumper |
|---|---|---|---|---|---|---|---|
| shirt | shoes | shorts | skirt | trainers | trousers | ~~T-shirt~~ | |

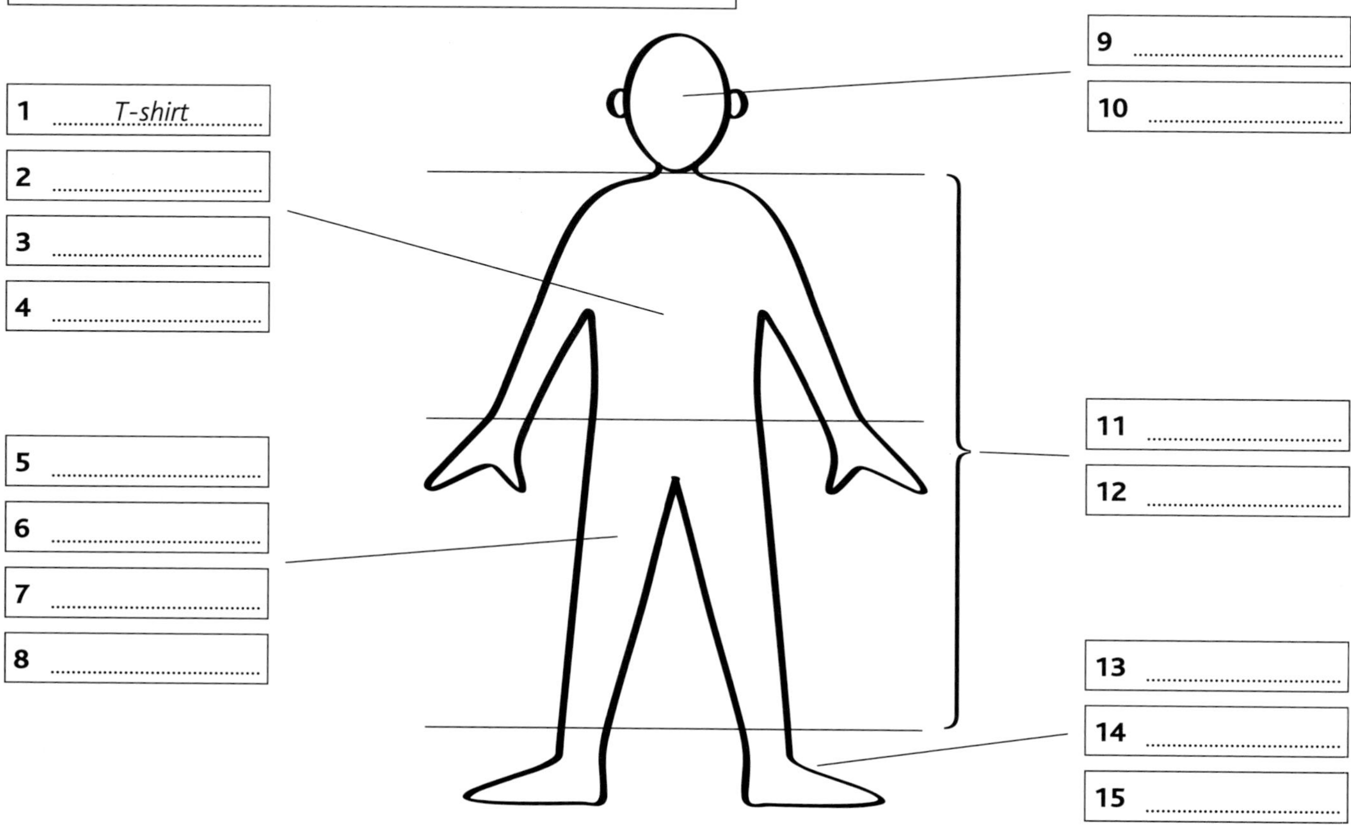


## Grammar: *have got*

**2 Complete the dialogues with the correct form of *have got*.**

1 A: *Have* you *got* your skateboard, Kelly?
B: Yes, I *have*.

2 A: .......... you .......... a computer?
B: No, I ........... But I .......... a mobile phone.

3 A: I .......... a new bike.
B: Great! I .......... a new bike, too. Let's go to school on our bikes!

4 A: .......... you and your sister .......... a TV in your bedroom?
B: No we ........... But we .......... an MP3 player.

5 A: Mum, .......... we .......... any sandwiches?
B: Yes, we ........... They're on the table.

6 A: Come in! We .......... some new CDs. Listen to these!
B: .......... you .......... any Lady Gaga CDs?
A: No, we ........... Sorry!

## About you

**3 Write about the clothes you've got in your bedroom/wardrobe.**

- What clothes are they?
- What colour are they?

*I've got some white trainers and some blue jeans.*
*I've got …*

..................................................

..................................................

..................................................

..................................................

..................................................

..................................................

..................................................

..................................................

..................................................

..................................................

# B Foundation exercises



## Vocabulary: Hair

**1 Match the pictures with the phrases.**

1 short curly hair ...*d*...
2 short spiky hair .........
3 long curly hair .........
4 long straight hair .........
5 medium-length straight hair .........
6 medium-length wavy hair .........

**2 Write the letters in the correct order to make the hair colour words.**

1 baklc ...*black*...
2 bwonr .....................
3 erd .....................
4 bnelod .....................

## Grammar: *have got*

**3 Choose the correct words.**

1 (*Have*) / *Has* they got any presents?
2 They *haven't* / *hasn't* got any chocolate cakes.
3 They *'ve* / *'s* got some CDs.
4 *Have* / *Has* they got friends from Italy?
5 They *haven't* / *hasn't* got any sandwiches.
6 They *'ve* / *'s* got some apples and oranges.

**4 Complete the dialogues with *has* or *hasn't*.**

1 A: ...*Has*... she got a mobile phone?
B: Yes, she ...*has*....
2 A: ..................... she got any school books?
B: Yes, she .....................
3 A: ..................... he got any ice cream?
B: No, he .....................
4 A: ..................... he got any black trousers?
B: No, he .....................
5 A: ..................... she got her coat?
B: No, she .....................
6 A: ..................... he got his MP3 player?
B: Yes, he .....................

# B Activation exercises

## Vocabulary: Hair

**1 Write the hair words.**

curly long medium-length
medium-length ~~short~~
~~spiky~~ straight wavy

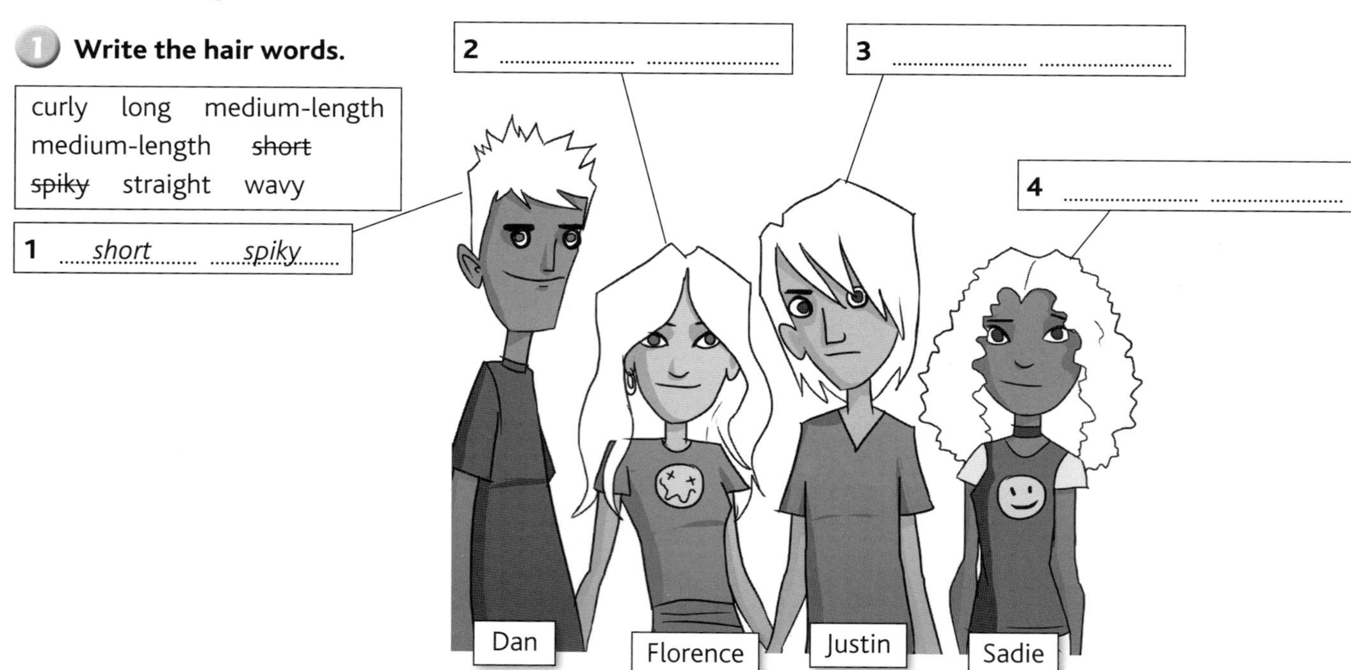


**2 Look at the picture in Exercise 1. Read and colour their hair.**

1 Dan has got black hair.
2 Florence has got brown hair.
3 Justin has got blonde hair.
4 Sadie has got red hair.

## Grammar: *have got*

**3 Look at the picture in Exercise 1. Read and answer *True* (*T*) or *False* (*F*).**

1 Dan's got short black hair. T
2 Sadie's got curly red hair. ☐
3 Florence has got short wavy hair. ☐
4 Justin's got straight black hair. ☐
5 Dan's got black spiky hair. ☐
6 Florence has got short brown hair. ☐

**4 Write sentences about the people in Exercise 1.**

1 Dan / (✗) long black hair
*Dan hasn't got long black hair.*
2 Sadie / (✗) short blonde hair
..............................
3 Justin / (✓) medium-length blonde hair
..............................
4 Justin / (✗) long wavy hair
..............................
5 Dan / (✓) short spiky hair
..............................
6 Florence / (✓) long wavy hair
..............................
7 Florence / (✗) long blonde hair
..............................
8 Sadie / (✓) medium-length red hair
..............................

**5 Look at the table and answer the questions.**

| | jacket | cap | trainers | mobile phone | MP3 player |
|---|---|---|---|---|---|
| Megan | ✗ | ✓ | ✓ | ✗ | ✓ |
| Will | ✗ | ✓ | ✓ | ✓ | ✗ |

1 Has Megan got an MP3 player? *Yes, she has.*
2 Has Will got a mobile phone? ..............
3 Have Megan and Will got trainers? ..............
4 Has Megan got a mobile phone? ..............
5 Has Will got an MP3 player? ..............
6 Have Megan and Will got caps? ..............
7 Have Megan and Will got jackets? ..............

**6 Who is it? Find the correct stickers.**

1 She's got short black spiky hair.
2 She's got long straight red hair.
3 He's got short curly black hair.

4 He's got medium-length red wavy hair.
5 She's got long straight blonde hair.
6 He's got long blonde wavy hair.

**7 Read the text and complete the fact file.**

*Justin Bieber is my favourite pop star and actor. He isn't from the USA – he's from Canada. He's got straight medium-length blonde hair. Has he got blue eyes? No, he hasn't! His eyes are brown.*

**Fact file**

| | |
|---|---|
| Name | 1 *Justin Bieber* |
| Country | 2 ........................ |
| Job | 3 ........................ |
| Hair | 4 ........................ |
| Eyes | 5 ........................ |

**8 Look at the fact file in Exercise 7 and answer the questions.**

1 What's his name? *Justin Bieber.*
2 Is he from the USA? ........................
3 Is he an actor? ........................
4 Has he got black hair? ........................
5 Has he got wavy hair? ........................
6 Has he got brown eyes? ........................

## English today

**9 Complete Mia's blog.**

| Bye for | Check out | Got to | ~~fantastic~~ |
|---|---|---|---|

**Hi!** This is my new English blog. My name's Mia and I've got two brothers, Paolo and Vincenzo. We're from Italy. It's my birthday today and I've got a new computer – it's 1 *fantastic* !

Paolo's got a new bike. 2 ........................ the photos in blog number 2!

It's now eight o'clock – time to go to school. 3 ........................ go!

4 ........................ now!

*Mia*

# B Extension exercises

## Vocabulary: Hair

**1 Find eleven hair words.**

| | | | | | | | | | | | |
|---|---|---|---|---|---|---|---|---|---|---|---|
| W | A | V | Y | I | M | N | A | H | M | E | L |
| P | I | C | E | T | S | L | L | R | N | Y | Y |
| O | T | U | E | R | P | R | O | D | B | S | P |
| T | L | R | E | D | I | S | O | U | R | T | D |
| A | B | L | A | C | K | L | S | H | O | R | T |
| N | L | Y | M | T | Y | D | R | N | W | A | R |
| L | O | N | G | R | T | R | L | S | N | I | R |
| Y | N | I | O | M | S | R | B | Y | E | G | L |
| R | D | E | S | N | P | K | I | R | N | H | H |
| M | E | D | I | U | M | L | E | N | G | T | H |

**2 Write the words from Exercise 1 in the correct columns.**

| | |
|---|---|
| Length | ..........<br>..........<br>.......... |
| Colour | ..........<br>..........<br>..........<br>.......... |
| Style | *wavy*<br>..........<br>..........<br>.......... |

**3 Write about Mark and Megan's hair and eyes.**

..........

..........

..........

## Grammar: *have got*

**4 Read the text and answer the questions.**

Hello, I'm Gina. I'm twelve years old and I'm from Italy. I've got brown eyes and long brown hair. I've got a sister, Lucia, and a brother, Leonardo. They've got brown eyes, too. Lucia's fourteen. She's got medium-length black hair. Leonardo is seventeen and he's got short brown hair. My mum and dad have got short black hair and brown eyes. They're thirty-eight years old.

1 Has Gina got green eyes?
*No, she hasn't. She's got brown eyes.*

2 Has she got black hair?
..........

3 Has she got long hair?
..........

4 Have her brother and sister got green eyes?
..........

5 Has her sister got medium-length hair?
..........

6 Has her brother got short hair?
..........

7 Have her mum and dad got blue eyes?
..........

8 Has her mum got long hair?
..........

## About you

**5 Describe yourself and your family. Use Exercise 4 to help you.**

..........

..........

..........

..........

..........

..........

## Speaking: Describe people

**1 Write the words in the correct order.**

1 got | hair | she's | short

*She's got short hair.*

2 she | hair? | has | long | got

..................................................

3 got? | colour | has | she | eyes | what

..................................................

4 colour | she | hair | what | has | got?

..................................................

### Your turn

**2 Complete the dialogue with the sentences from Exercise 1.**

*Olivia and her mum are at the airport to meet Olivia's friend for the first time.*

**Mum:** What's your friend's name?
**Olivia:** Sophie.
**Mum:** 1 ..................................................
**Olivia:** She's got blonde hair.
**Mum:** OK. 2 ..................................................
**Olivia:** Her eyes are green.
**Mum:** Blonde with green eyes.
3 ..................................................
**Olivia:** No, she hasn't. 4 ..................................................
**Mum:** Has she got a brown bag?
**Olivia:** I'm not sure.
**Mum:** Have your got your phone? Why don't you call her?
**Olivia:** OK!

## Writing: Describe a character

**3 Complete the text with *and* and *but*.**

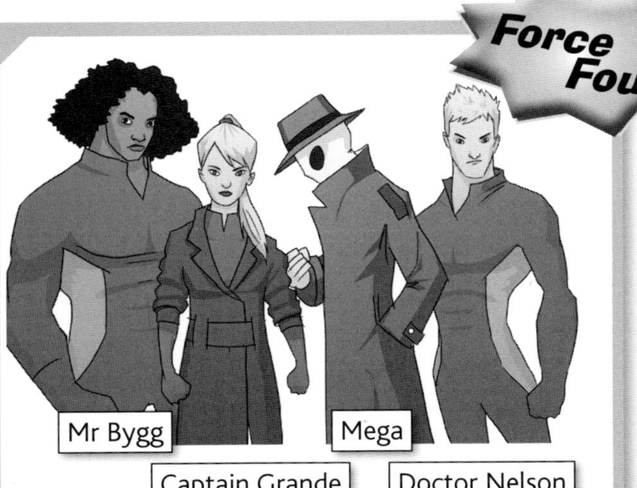


This is my favourite video game, *Force Four*. The four characters are great! Doctor Nelson has got short blonde hair 1 *and* blue eyes. Captain Grande is his sister. She's got long blonde hair 2 .......... she hasn't got blue eyes – her eyes are brown. Mr Bygg has got curly black hair 3 .......... brown eyes. My favourite character is Mega – he's white 4 .......... he's got big black eyes. He's got a black coat 5 .......... a black hat 6 .......... he hasn't got a jacket.

### Your turn

**4 Write about characters from your favourite film, TV programme or video game. Use *and* and *but*. Use Exercise 3 to help you.**

..................................................
..................................................
..................................................
..................................................
..................................................
..................................................
..................................................
..................................................
..................................................

# Check

**1 Choose the correct words.**

Andy Murray and Novak Djokovic are very good tennis players but they are friends, too. We [1] *'ve* / *'s* got a photo here. Andy [2] *'ve* / *'s* got brown curly hair but Novak [3] *haven't* / *hasn't* got curly hair – he [4] *'ve* / *'s* got short straight black hair. In the photo, [5] they *'ve* / *'s* got T-shirts. Andy [6] *have* / *has* got a grey T-shirt but Novak [7] *have* / *has* got a white T-shirt. They [8] *haven't* / *hasn't* got their caps today.

**Score:** ........ /7

**2 Write the words in the correct columns.**

blonde ~~boots~~ jumper medium-length shorts skirt spiky trousers wavy

| Clothes | Hair |
|---|---|
| *boots* | ........ |
| ........ | ........ |
| ........ | ........ |
| ........ | ........ |
| ........ | |

**Score:** ........ /8

**Colour one ring on Lenny's tail for each correct answer.**

My score is ..................!

# 5 Routines

## A Foundation exercises

### Vocabulary: Routine activities

**1 Complete Busy Beth's speech bubbles.**

| do | ~~get up~~ | go | have | play | play |
|---|---|---|---|---|---|

1 I ......*get up*...... at six o'clock.
2 I .................... breakfast at half past six.
3 I .................... to school at quarter to eight.
4 I .................... football at half past three.
5 I .................... my homework at six o'clock.
6 I .................... computer games at half past seven.
Corn Flakes
GAME


**2 Look at the pictures in Exercise 1 and complete the sentences.**

1 Busy Beth ......*gets up*...... at six o'clock.
2 She .............................. at half past six.
3 She .............................. at quarter to eight.
4 She .............................. at half past three.
5 She .................. her .................. at six o'clock.
6 She .............................. at half past seven.

### Grammar: Present simple; Adverbs of frequency

**3 Choose the correct words.**

1 I (*get*) / *gets* up at half past six.
2 She *go* / *goes* to school at quarter to eight.
3 We *do* / *does* our homework at six o'clock.
4 He *have* / *has* dinner at seven o'clock.
5 I *start* / *starts* school at half past eight.

**4 Complete the sentences.**

| always | 100% |
|---|---|
| usually | 90% |
| often | 70% |
| sometimes | 50% |
| never | 0% |

1 They (90%) ......*usually*...... have dinner at seven o'clock.
2 You (0%) .................... do your homework on Saturday.
3 We (50%) .................... go to school by bus.
4 He (70%) .................... watches TV in his bedroom.
5 I (100%) .................... have breakfast at seven o'clock.
6 She (50%) .................... plays football with her brother.

# A Activation exercises

## Vocabulary: Routine activities

**1 Complete the phrases.**

| dinner football ~~school~~ school to school up |
|---|

1 finish *school*
2 play ..........
3 go ..........
4 have ..........
5 start ..........
6 get ..........

**2 Find the correct stickers.**

1 I do my homework in my bedroom.

2 I get dressed at quarter to seven in the morning.

3 I have breakfast in the kitchen.

4 I go to bed at half past ten.

5 I watch TV in bed in the evening.

6 I play computer games in the afternoon.

## Grammar: Present simple; Adverbs of frequency

**3 Look at Exercise 2 and complete the sentences.**

1 He *does his homework* in his bedroom.
2 He .......... at quarter to seven in the morning.
3 He .......... in the kitchen.
4 He .......... at half past ten.
5 He .......... in the evening.
6 He .......... in the afternoon.

**4 Choose the correct words.**

1 We (*have*) / *has* cereal for breakfast.
2 My brother and I *play / plays* computer games in our room.
3 Tom *do / does* his homework in his bedroom.
4 I *have / has* an apple and a banana for lunch.
5 Katie *watch / watches* TV at seven o'clock.
6 Mum and Dad *have / has* lunch in the kitchen.

**5 Write the adverbs in the triangle.**

| ~~always~~ never often sometimes usually |
|---|

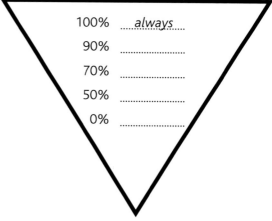

100% *always*
90% ..........
70% ..........
50% ..........
0% ..........

**6 Complete the sentences about you. Use the adverbs in Exercise 5.**

1 I .......... have cereal for breakfast.
2 I .......... play football at the weekend.
3 I .......... watch TV after school.
4 I .......... do my homework.

## 7 Write the words in the correct order.

1 finish | school | we | always | at | four o'clock

*We always finish school at four o'clock.*

2 watches | sometimes | she | in her room | TV

3 often | has | he | sandwiches | for lunch

4 go | never | you | at | ten o'clock | to bed

5 go | usually | at | eight o'clock | to | school | they

6 Mum | at | gets up | always | six o'clock

7 I | computer games | play | never

8 often | has | for breakfast | a banana | my brother

## 8 Read and answer *True* (*T*) or *False* (*F*).

### Darren's blog

My favourite sport is basketball and I play it every Saturday morning. My favourite basketball player is Kobe Bryant. He's from the USA and he's awesome! Here's his routine every day.

He gets up at half past seven every morning and he has breakfast. He always has cereal and an orange. Sometimes he has a banana, too. He gets dressed for basketball – his favourite clothes are his T-shirt, shorts and trainers. He always plays basketball in the morning and then he has lunch. He usually has a sandwich. In the afternoon he goes to bed – he always sleeps for two hours. On Tuesday and Saturday evenings he plays in a basketball match. He often listens to music before the match and he always talks to the players.

Darren

1 Darren plays basketball every Saturday. T
2 Kobe Bryant is American. ☐
3 Kobe gets up at 7.30. ☐
4 He has cereal for breakfast. ☐
5 He never has a banana for breakfast. ☐
6 He never plays basketball in the mornings. ☐
7 He always has a sandwich for lunch. ☐
8 He always sleeps in the afternoon. ☐
9 He plays in matches two days every week. ☐
10 He never listens to music before the match. ☐

## 9 Look at Exercise 8 and write sentences about Kobe Bryant's routine.

*I get up at half past seven every morning and I have breakfast.*

## 10 Write a blog about your favourite player. Use the words in the box and Exercise 8 to help you.

| always | dinner | gets up | never |
|---|---|---|---|
| plays | sometimes | usually | |

*My favourite player is* ..........

*He/She* ..........

# A Extension exercises

## Vocabulary: Routine activities

**1 Complete the table. Write the verbs for the words.**

| | |
|---|---|
| 1 ......do...... | homework |
| 2 ...................... | to bed<br>to school |
| 3 ......................<br>4 ...................... | school |
| 5 ...................... | breakfast<br>lunch<br>dinner |
| 6 ...................... | football<br>computer games |
| 7 ...................... | TV |
| 8 ...................... | dressed<br>up |

**2 Put the activities in the correct order for you. Then write sentences with the times.**

a [2] have breakfast [1] get up

*I get up at half past six.*

*I have breakfast at quarter to seven.*

b [ ] get dressed [ ] have breakfast

..................................................

..................................................

c [ ] start school [ ] go to school

..................................................

..................................................

d [ ] have lunch [ ] finish school

..................................................

..................................................

e [ ] watch TV [ ] do my homework

..................................................

..................................................

f [ ] have dinner [ ] go to bed

..................................................

..................................................

## Grammar: Present simple; Adverbs of frequency

**3 Complete the text.**

*Hi! I'm Flavia. This is my family's Saturday routine. I [1] ...get up... (get up) at eight o'clock and I [2] ................ (have) breakfast with my family at half past eight. We [3] ................ (have) cereal but my sister usually [4] ................ (have) some apples, too. She [5] ................ (go) to school on Saturday – she [6] ................ (play) football. I [7] ................ (go) to my friend's house and we [8] ................ (listen) to music and [9] ................ (watch) TV. Sometimes we [10] ................ (play) computer games.*

**4 Write sentences.**

1 they / go / school / Saturday mornings (often)

*They often go to school on Saturday mornings.*

2 Peter / play / computer games / his room (never)

..................................................

3 Josh / have / lunch / school (always)

..................................................

4 Lucy / get up / late (sometimes)

..................................................

5 I / go / to bed / eleven o'clock (often)

..................................................

6 my parents / have / dinner / kitchen (usually)

..................................................

### About you

**5 Write about two people in your family. Use Exercise 3 to help you.**

*My mum always gets up at half past six in the morning and my brother gets up at quarter to seven. They usually have breakfast at seven o'clock.*

..................................................

..................................................

..................................................

..................................................

..................................................

## Vocabulary: School subjects

**1 Write the school subjects.**

| Art | English | ICT | ~~Maths~~ | Science |
|---|---|---|---|---|

Hello! I'm Emma.

Hi! I'm George.

1 ........*Maths*........
2 ..............................
3 ..............................
4 ..............................
5 ..............................

**2 Complete the school subjects.**

1 Ph*y*sical E*d*ucation
2 Ge....gra....hy
3 Re....igious E....ucatio....
4 H....st....ry
5 Fre.... .... ....

## Grammar: Present simple

**3 Choose the correct words.**

1 **A:** Do you have English on Wednesdays?
**B:** Yes, I *(do)* / *don't*.
2 **A:** Do they play football every day?
**B:** No, they *do* / *don't*.
3 **A:** Do you do your homework in the afternoon?
**B:** No, we *do* / *don't*.
4 **A:** Do you have History today?
**B:** Yes, I *do* / *don't*.
5 **A:** Do Megan and Mark go to school on Saturdays?
**B:** No, they *do* / *don't*.
6 **A:** Do you have Maths on Thursdays?
**B:** Yes, we *do* / *don't*.

**4 Complete the dialogues with *do*, *does*, *don't* or *doesn't*.**

1 **A:** Does Sarah play ice hockey?
**B:** Yes, she ....*does*.....
2 **A:** Do Will and Megan go to school on Sundays?
**B:** No, they .....................
3 **A:** Do you have Science on Fridays?
**B:** No, we .....................
4 **A:** Does Sarah's brother play in the team?
**B:** Yes, he .....................
5 **A:** Do you play basketball?
**B:** Yes, I .....................
6 **A:** Does Mark have Maths on Tuesdays?
**B:** No, he .....................

# B Activation exercises

## Vocabulary: School subjects

**1 Write the school subjects.**

1 ......*ICT*......

2 ..............................

3 ..............................

4 ..............................

5 ..............................

6 ..............................

**2 Write the school subjects.**

Bonjour, François! Ça va?

1 ..............................

France and Spain are in Europe.

2 ..............................

Draw a picture of your family.

3 ..............................

## Grammar: Present simple

**3 (3 05) Listen and choose the correct school subjects for Joe.**

**Joe's timetable**

| | Morning | Afternoon |
|---|---|---|
| Monday | 1 (ICT) / Geography<br>2 History / Maths | 3 RE / PE |
| Tuesday | 4 French / RE<br>5 English / Art | 6 ICT / Science |
| Wednesday | 7 Art / English<br>8 Science / Maths | 9 History / PE |

**4 Choose the correct words.**

**Keith:** Hi, Nina! What subjects 1 (*do*) / *does* you have today?
**Nina:** I have Art, PE and RE. And you?
**Keith:** I have Maths, Science and English.
**Nina:** Bad luck!
**Keith:** It's OK. I like those subjects. 2 *Do / Does* you have English on Thursdays?
**Nina:** No, I 3 *don't / doesn't*. I have English on Tuesdays, Wednesdays and Fridays.
**Keith:** 4 *Don't / Does* your brother have English on those days, too?
**Nina:** No, he 5 *does / doesn't*. He has English on Mondays and Thursdays.
**Keith:** 6 *Do / Does* we have lunch now?
**Nina:** Yes, we 7 *do / does*. It's five to one. Let's go!

## 5 Read the text and answer the questions.

David Harvey is eighteen and he's from Canada. He plays for a Canadian ice hockey team. Sport is in his family – his dad plays ice hockey, too, and his mum plays tennis.

David doesn't go to school now but he has French lessons every Monday and Thursday afternoon. Every morning he has ice hockey practice and talks to the team players. They have ice hockey matches every Tuesday and Friday evening. He always goes to bed at eleven o'clock and he sleeps for eight hours. He doesn't play on Saturday and Sunday afternoons – he usually goes to his friend's house and they sometimes listen to music.

1 Does David play for a Canadian ice hockey team?
*Yes, he does.*
2 Do his mum and dad play sports?
..........
3 Does David go to school?
..........
4 Does he have English lessons?
..........
5 Does he have practice every morning?
..........
6 Does he have matches on Saturdays?
..........
7 Does he go to bed at eleven o'clock?
..........
8 Does he sleep for eight hours?
..........
9 Do his friends watch TV on Sunday afternoons?
..........

## English today

### 6 Complete the dialogue.

| Bad | Good night | night | ~~do we~~ |
|---|---|---|---|

**Sam:** Hi, Kelly and Katie! I've got Maths homework.
**Kelly and Katie:** So [1] *do we*! We have Maths lessons every Monday at school.
**Sam:** [2] .......... luck!
**Kelly and Katie:** It's OK. On Tuesdays we have Art and PE.
**Sam:** That's good! OK, time to go. Night [3] ..........!
**Kelly and Katie:** [4] .........., Sam!

### 7 Write questions.

1 You have Maths every day.
*Do you have Maths every day?*
2 Your dad has lunch at one o'clock.
..........
3 You have Science on Fridays.
..........
4 You and your friend have lunch at school.
..........
5 Your friend plays football.
..........
6 You play basketball.
..........
7 Your cousins have English lessons.
..........

## About you

### 8 Answer the questions in Exercise 7 about you.

1 *Yes, I do. / No, I don't.*
2 ..........
3 ..........
4 ..........
5 ..........
6 ..........
7 ..........

# B Extension exercises

## Vocabulary: School subjects

**1 Write the letters in the correct order to make the school subjects and complete the crossword.**

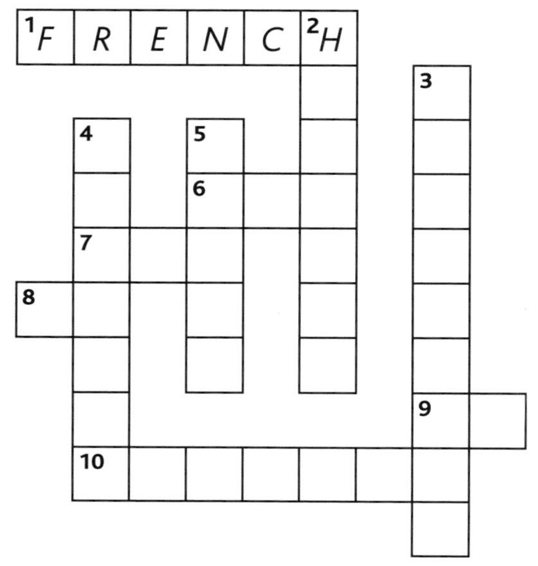


1 enhFcr
2 styiHro
3 ogphayeGr
4 iecSecn
5 stMah
6 rtA
7 CTI
8 ER
9 EP
10 gihEnls

## Grammar: Present simple

**2 Answer the questions about you.**

1 Do you have English every day?
*Yes, I do. / No, I don't.*

2 Do you have Geography on Fridays?
..........

3 Does your friend have lunch at school?
..........

4 Do you and your friend play computer games every day?
..........

5 Do you have PE on Mondays?
..........

6 Do you play in a team?
..........

7 Does your friend play in a team?
..........

8 Does your dad play computer games?
..........

**3 Read the text and choose the correct words. Then answer the questions.**

Hi! My name's Santiago. I'm from Argentina but my home is in London, in the UK. I start school at half past eight in the morning. I have Maths and English on Monday, Wednesday and Friday mornings. My favourite day is Tuesday – we have Art and ICT in the morning and PE in the afternoon. Thursday isn't a good day for me – we have Geography and French! Every afternoon I play in the school football team with my friends Freddie and Michael.

1 *Do* / *Does* Santiago come from the USA?
*No, he doesn't.*

2 *Do* / *Does* he go to school in the mornings?
..........

3 *Do* / *Does* he have Maths on Tuesdays?
..........

4 *Do* / *Does* he have ICT on Tuesdays?
..........

5 *Do* / *Does* he play football for the school team?
..........

6 *Do* / *Does* his friends play for the team, too?
..........

**4 Write about your school timetable and your favourite day. Use Exercise 3 to help you.**

..........

**5 Write two questions for your friend about his/her school timetable.**

*Do you have English on Fridays?*

1 ..........

2 ..........

## Vocabulary: Jobs and places of work

**1 Choose the correct words for 1–9 in the table.**

| | Job | Place of work |
|---|---|---|
| | [1] (waiter) / doctor | A *restaurant* |
| | [2] vet / chef | B ........ |
| | [3] hairdresser / shop assistant | C ........ |
| | [4] mechanic / secretary | D ........ |
| | [5] receptionist / vet | E ........ |

| | Job | Place of work |
|---|---|---|
| | [6] waiter / secretary | F ........ |
| | [7] receptionist / chef | G ........ |
| | [8] shop assistant / hairdresser | H ........ |
| | [9] doctor / mechanic | I ........ |

**2 Write the places of work in A–I in the table in Exercise 1.**

animal hospital garage hospital hotel office ~~restaurant~~ restaurant salon shop

## Grammar: Present simple

**3 Match the questions with the answers.**

1 What do you do? — d
2 What time do you start work?
3 What do you wear for work?
4 Where do you work?
5 What does she do?
6 Where does he work?

a She's a shop assistant.
b He works in a garage.
c In a hotel.
d I'm a doctor.
e At half past eight.
f Jeans and a T-shirt.

**4 Choose the correct words.**

1 I (*don't*) / *does* work in a hotel.
2 What time *do / does* you start work?
3 She *does / doesn't* start at eight o'clock.
4 *Do / Doesn't* you work in a salon?
5 Where *do / does* she work?
6 They *don't / doesn't* work on Mondays.

# C Activation exercises

## Vocabulary: Jobs and places of work

**1 Write the letters in the correct order to make the places of work.**

1 oehlt ........*hotel*........
2 ragaeg ....................
3 fiecfo ....................
4 spalhoit ....................
5 stranreaut ....................
6 imanla pithalos ....................
7 loasn ....................
8 phos ....................

**2 Read and write the jobs.**

1 He works in a salon. ........*hairdresser*........
2 She works in a hospital. ....................
3 She works in an animal hospital. ....................
4 He works in a hotel. ....................
5 He works in a restaurant. He doesn't work in the kitchen. ....................
6 She works in a garage. ....................
7 He works in a restaurant, in the kitchen. ....................
8 He works in a shop. ....................
9 She works in an office. ....................

## Grammar: Present simple

**3 Choose the correct words.**

1 *Who* / *What* (circled) time do you finish work?
2 *What* / *Where* does he work?
3 *What* / *Where* do you do?
4 *What time* / *What* do they wear for work?
5 *What* / *Where* do you go to school?
6 *What time* / *What* do they start school?

**4 Read Lottie's answers and complete Emmy's email. Use some words more than once.**

| What ...? | What time ...? | Where ...? |
|---|---|---|

**To:** Emmy
**From:** Lottie
**Subject:** Re: Hello!

Hi, Emmy!

Thanks for your email and your questions! Here are my answers:

1 I go to school in Northgate, in London.
2 I start lessons at nine o'clock.
3 I wear a skirt and shirt and a jumper for school.
4 My dad's a doctor.
5 He works in a hospital.
6 My mum's a receptionist.
7 She works in a hotel.

Do you watch TV? I watch TV every evening. My favourite TV programme is *Animal Hospital*. What's your favourite TV programme?

Bye for now!

Lottie

---

From: Emmy

Hi, Lottie! I have some questions for you!

1 *Where do you go to school?*
2 ....................
3 ....................
4 ....................
5 ....................
6 ....................
7 ....................

Write soon! Bye!

Emmy

## 5 Choose the correct answers.

*Today SixTEEN is with Jason Raymond. He's twenty-six years old and he's a [1] ...... Let's meet him!*

**SixTEEN**: Hello, Jason. You've got an interesting job.
**Jason**: Yes, it's cool!
**SixTEEN**: Where do you [2] ......?
**Jason**: I [3] ...... in my aunt's [4] ...... in Manchester.
**SixTEEN**: [5] ...... your aunt work in the salon?
**Jason**: Yes she [6] ......! She's always here early in the morning. She [7] ...... work at half past seven.
**SixTEEN**: What time [8] ...... you start work?
**Jason**: I [9] ...... at half past eight and I [10] ...... at four o'clock.
**SixTEEN**: Half past eight is early!
**Jason**: Yes, but it's OK. My job is great!
**SixTEEN**: Do you [11] ...... every day?
**Jason**: No. I [12] ...... work on Sundays and Mondays.
**SixTEEN**: Today is Monday and you're at work! Sorry, Jason!

1 a waiter (b) hairdresser
2 a work b works
3 a work b works
4 a salon b hotel
5 a Do b Does
6 a do b does
7 a start b starts
8 a do b does
9 a start b starts
10 a finish b finishes
11 a work b works
12 a don't b doesn't

## 6 Complete the text about Jason. Use Exercise 5 to help you.

Today we meet Jason Raymond. He's twenty-six years old and he's a hairdresser. He [1] *works* in his aunt's salon in Manchester. His aunt [2] ........ in the salon, too. She always [3] ........ work early – at half past seven in the morning. Jason [4] ........ work at half past eight and he [5] ........ at four o'clock. He [6] ........ work every day. He doesn't [7] ........ on Sundays and Mondays.

## 7 Read the text about Jason's sister and answer the questions.

Daisy is Jason's sister. She's twenty years old and she works in an office in Manchester. She's a secretary. She wears a dress and shoes at work but at home she wears jeans and a jumper. Daisy starts work at nine o'clock in the morning and finishes at five o'clock in the afternoon. She doesn't work every day. She's at home on Saturdays and Sundays.

1 Who is Daisy?
*She's Jason's sister.*
2 How old is Daisy?
........
3 Where does she work?
........
4 What does she wear at work?
........
5 What time does she start work?
........
6 What time does she finish work?
........
7 Does she work every day?
........
8 Where is she on Saturdays and Sundays?
........

# C Extension exercises

## Vocabulary: Jobs and places of work

**1 Match the letters. Make six jobs and six places of work.**

~~doc~~ mech off sec hosp hot gar wait sal hair rest recep

age dresser on anic ice el ital aurant ~~tor~~ er tionist retary

1 ......*doctor*...... 4 ............ 7 ............ 10 ............
2 ............ 5 ............ 8 ............ 11 ............
3 ............ 6 ............ 9 ............ 12 ............

**2 Answer the questions.**

1 Where does a chef work?

*In a* ............

2 What colour are a chef's clothes, usually?

............

3 Where does a mechanic work?

............

4 What time do shop assistants start work in your country?

............

5 Where does a vet work?

............

6 What does a waiter wear for work?

............

**3 Write the jobs and places of work from Exercises 1 and 2 in the correct columns.**

| Jobs | Places of work |
|---|---|
| ......*Doctor*...... | ............ |
| ............ | ............ |
| ............ | ............ |
| ............ | ............ |
| ............ | ............ |
| ............ | ............ |
| ............ | ............ |
| ............ | |
| ............ | |

## Grammar: Present simple

**4 Complete the dialogue. What does Bill do?**

**Amy:** [1] ...*What time*... do you start work?
**Bill:** I always [2] ............ work at seven o'clock in the morning.
**Amy:** And what time [3] ............ finish work?
**Bill:** I usually [4] ............ work at eleven o'clock in the evening!
**Amy:** [5] ............ do you [6] ............ for work?
**Bill:** I wear blue and white trousers, a white shirt and a white hat.
**Amy:** And where do [7] ............?
**Bill:** I [8] ............ in a restaurant.
**Amy:** Do [9] ............ in the kitchen?
**Bill:** Yes, I do.
**Amy:** And [10] ............'s your job?
**Bill:** I'm a [11] ............ .

### About you

**5 Write a dialogue with someone in your family about his/her job. Use Exercise 4 to help you.**

You: ............
............: ............
You: ............
............: ............
You: ............
............: ............
You: ............
............: ............
You: ............
............: ............
You: ............
............: ............

## Speaking: Give invitations

**1 Write the phrases in the correct box.**

Are you free on Saturday? Great! See you soon! Sorry, I can't. I'm busy. ~~Sure!~~
That's a pity. Would you like to come ...? Yes, that sounds fun/good/great.

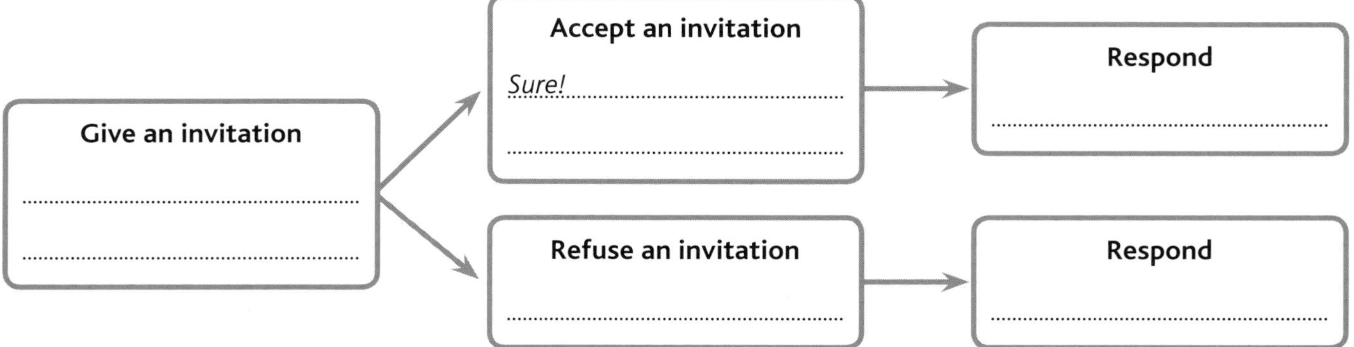


### Your turn

**2 Complete the dialogue. Use phrases from Exercise 1.**

**Mark:** Hi, Will! Are [1] *you free on Saturday* ?
I've got some great new CDs.

**Will:** Sorry, Mark, I [2] .................................
I've got football practice with the school team.

**Mark:** Oh, that's a [3] .................................
And we have burgers for lunch – they're your favourite!

**Will:** Oh, that [4] ................................. great!
But never mind.

**Mark:** Would you [5] ................................. on Sunday?

**Will:** Sure! Do you have burgers on Sunday, too?

**Mark:** No, we don't. We have sandwiches for lunch.

**Will:** That's OK. [6] ................................. you on Sunday!

## Writing: A party invitation

**3 Write the headings. Use *Date*, *Place*, *Time* or *To*.**

1 *Place* 34, Poolside Road
2 .......... Will Taylor
3 .......... Tuesday 6th January
4 .......... 12, High Street
5 .......... 2 o'clock–5 o'clock
6 .......... Amy Price
7 .......... 5 o'clock–8 o'clock
8 .......... Saturday 30th September

### Your turn

**4 Complete the invitation.**

16, Rowling Road 9 p.m. Friday Love
Please come to ~~Sophie Lewis~~ the right clothes

IT'S A PARTY!
To: [1] *Sophie Lewis*
[2] .......................... my 'Jobs' party!
Date: [3] .......................... 7th November
Time: 6 p.m.– [4] ..........................
Place: My house – [5] ..........................
Wear [6] .......................... for your job!
See you soon!
[7] ..........................,
Drew

# Check

**1 Complete Polly's blog.**

| ~~do I go~~ | doesn't work | don't go | don't have | have | have | play | plays | works |
|---|---|---|---|---|---|---|---|---|

Where [1] *do I go* to school? At home! My brother (Josh) and I [2] .................... to a school. We [3] .................... our lessons here. My mum's usually a **secretary** but she's my teacher, too. My dad's usually a Maths **teacher** – he [4] .................... in a school but he's my teacher at home, too.

My brother and I [5] .................... **Maths** and **English** on Tuesday and Thursday mornings, 8.30 a.m.–11.30 a.m. On Monday and Friday mornings we have **RE**, Geography, French and History. Then in the afternoons (1.30 p.m.–4.30 p.m.) we have Art, Science, PE and **ICT**. We [6] .................... lessons on Wednesdays – it's our day off! On Saturday my dad [7] .................... at school, and we **have lessons** at home in the morning. I [8] .................... **basketball** with my friends on Saturday afternoon and my brother [9] .................... football.

Polly

**Score:** ........ /8

**2 Look at the words in bold in Exercise 1. Write them in the correct columns.**

| Routine activities | Subjects | Jobs |
|---|---|---|
| .................... | *Maths* | .................... |
| .................... | .................... | .................... |
| | .................... | |
| | .................... | |

**Score:** ........ /7

**Colour one ring on Lenny's tail for each correct answer.**

My score is ..................!

# 6 Outside

## A Foundation exercises

### Vocabulary: Places in town

**1 Complete the places.**

1 boo*k* sh*o*p

2 po.....t of.....ice

3 cin.....ma

4 ne.....sag.....nt's

5 swi.....ming p.....ol

6 ca.....é

7 sta.....ion

8 spo.....ts ce.....tre

**2 Match the letters to make four places. Then write.**

| | | |
|---|---|---|
| 1 | music | market |
| 2 | shopping | pool |
| 3 | super | centre |
| 4 | swimming | shop |

1 *music shop*
2 ..............................
3 ..............................
4 ..............................

### Grammar: *How often do you ...?*; Time expressions

**3 Complete the answers with *once*, *twice*, *three times* or *four times*.**

How often do you go to computer classes?

1 Jerry: I go *twice* (2×) a week.
2 Maria: I go .............................. (3×) a week.
3 Letty: I go .............................. (1×) a week.
4 Sam: I go .............................. (2×) a month.
5 Harry: I go .............................. (4×) a week.
6 Kelly: I go .............................. (1×) a month.

**4 Choose the correct words.**

1 **A:** How *often* / *every* do you visit your aunt and uncle?
**B:** Twice a month.

2 **A:** How often do you practise football?
**B:** Twice *a* / *any* week.

3 **A:** How often do you watch TV?
**B:** *Every* / *Once* evening.

4 **A:** *How* / *What* often do you and your brother have an English lesson?
**B:** Three times a week.

5 **A:** How often do you go to karate class?
**B:** Twice *a* / *the* week.

6 **A:** How *often* / *sometimes* do you play basketball?
**B:** Every Saturday.

# A Activation exercises

## Vocabulary: Places in town

**1 Find the correct stickers.**

1 station

2 sports centre

3 café

4 newsagent's

5 supermarket

6 post office

**2 Write the places.**

1 There are lots of shops here.
*shopping centre*

2 There are lots of CDs here.
..................................

3 We watch films here.
..................................

4 I go swimming here once a week.
..................................

5 There are lots of books here.
..................................

## Grammar: *How often do you … ?*; Time expressions

**3 3 06 Listen and choose the correct answers.**

1 Sophie goes to judo practice
   a four times a week. (b) twice a week.
2 Ben watches TV
   a three times a week. b every evening.
3 Maddie has piano lessons
   a twice a week. b three times a week.
4 Josh goes to the cinema
   a every morning. b every week.

**4 Look at Sheena's timetable and complete the sentences about her.**

*My activities*

| *by Sheena* | times a week | times a month | times a year |
|---|---|---|---|
| 1 go bowling | | 1x | |
| 2 play basketball | 2x | | |
| 3 go to the cinema | | | 4x |
| 4 have judo practice | | 2x | |
| 5 do my homework | 6x | | |
| 6 watch TV | 7x | | |
| 7 visit Grandma | | | 6x |
| 8 go to computer club | 1x | | |

1 I go bowling *once a month*.
2 I play basketball ..................................
3 I go to the cinema ..................................
4 I have judo practice ..................................
5 I do my homework ..................................
6 I watch TV ..................................
7 I visit Grandma ..................................
8 I go to computer club ..................................

## 5 Read the interview and complete the table.

*SixTEEN talks to Lang Lang, the Chinese star of the piano. He works in New York, in the USA.*

**SixTEEN:** How often do you play the piano, Lang Lang?
**LL:** I play every day, seven times a week.
**SixTEEN:** Do you watch TV?
**LL:** Yes, I do.
**SixTEEN:** How often?
**LL:** Every day!
**SixTEEN:** What's your favourite programme?
**LL:** I often watch a sports programme, *Sport Today*. It's on Monday, Wednesday and Sunday.
**SixTEEN:** How often do you go to the cinema?
**LL:** Once a year. I usually watch films at home.
**SixTEEN:** How often do you watch films?
**LL:** Twice a week, usually on Sunday and Thursday.
**SixTEEN:** How often do you listen to music?
**LL:** Every day! It's my job! I listen to music with my friends at home, too.

| What? | How often? | Which days? |
|---|---|---|
| 1 play the piano | *7x/week* | *every day* |
| 2 watch TV | .................... | .................... |
| 3 watch sports programmes | .................... | .................... |
| 4 go to the cinema | .................... | – |
| 5 watch films | .................... | .................... |
| 6 listen to music | .................... | .................... |

## 6 Look at the table in Exercise 5 and write sentences about Lang Lang.

1 *He plays the piano seven times a week, every day.*
2 ....................
3 ....................
4 ....................
5 ....................
6 ....................

## 7 Write questions.

1 **A:** (how often / you) *How often do you play football?*
**B:** I play football twice a week.

2 **A:** (how often / you) ....................
**B:** We have English lessons three times a week.

3 **A:** (how often /he) ....................
**B:** He watches TV every evening.

4 **A:** (how often / they) ....................
**B:** They have a karate tournament twice a year.

5 **A:** (which day / he) ....................
**B:** He has guitar lessons on Thursdays.

6 **A:** (which day / she) ....................
**B:** She chats to her cousin online on Sundays.

7 **A:** (how often / you) ....................
**B:** We visit our grandmother twice a month.

## English today

## 8 Complete the dialogue.

can say that again    you any good

**Eddie:** I've got tennis practice at five o'clock.
**Hannah:** Tennis? Are [1] ...................., Eddie?
**Sophie:** Any good? You [2] ....................! Eddie's the tennis club champion!

# A Extension exercises

## Vocabulary: Places in town

**1 Write the words that go together.**

| book | music | ~~shopping~~ | sports | swimming |
|---|---|---|---|---|

1 *shopping* ……… } centre
2 ………

3 ……… } shop
4 ………

5 ……… } pool

**2 Write the names of places in your town.**

1 a cinema: *the Rex*
2 a café: ………
3 a newsagent's: ………
4 a supermarket: ………
5 a station: ………

## Grammar: *How often do you …?*; Time expressions

**3 Answer the questions about you. Write a number and choose *week*, *month* or *year*.**

### YOU AND YOUR ROUTINES

**Tell us about you!**

1 How often do you do your homework?
*5* times a (*week*) / *month* / *year*

2 How often does your mum watch TV?
☐ times a *week* / *month* / *year*

3 How often does your family have a barbecue?
☐ times a *week* / *month* / *year*

4 How often do your friends have a party?
☐ times a *week* / *month* / *year*

5 How often do you have English lessons?
☐ times a *week* / *month* / *year*

6 How often do you and your friend chat online?
☐ times a *week* / *month* / *year*

7 How often do you and your friends go to the cinema?
☐ times a *week* / *month* / *year*

## About you

**4 Answer the questions in Exercise 3 about you.**

1 *I do my homework five times a week.*
2 ………
3 ………
4 ………
5 ………
6 ………
7 ………

**5 Write questions. Use *how often*. Then answer the questions about you.**

1 you | go to school?
*How often do you go to school?*
*I go to school five times a week.*

2 you | have a birthday?
………
………

3 your dad | go to work?
………
………

4 your friend | go to the sports centre?
………
………

5 you | do your homework?
………
………

6 you and your family | watch TV?
………
………

# B Foundation exercises 6

## Vocabulary: Months; Ordinal numbers 1–31

**1 Complete the months.**

| | | | | | |
|---|---|---|---|---|---|
| 1 January | 2 Febr......... | 3 Mar......... | 4 Apr......... | 5 Ma......... | 6 Jun......... |
| 7 Jul......... | 8 Augu......... | 9 Septem......... | 10 Oct......... | 11 Nove......... | 12 Dec......... |

**2 Match the numbers with the words.**

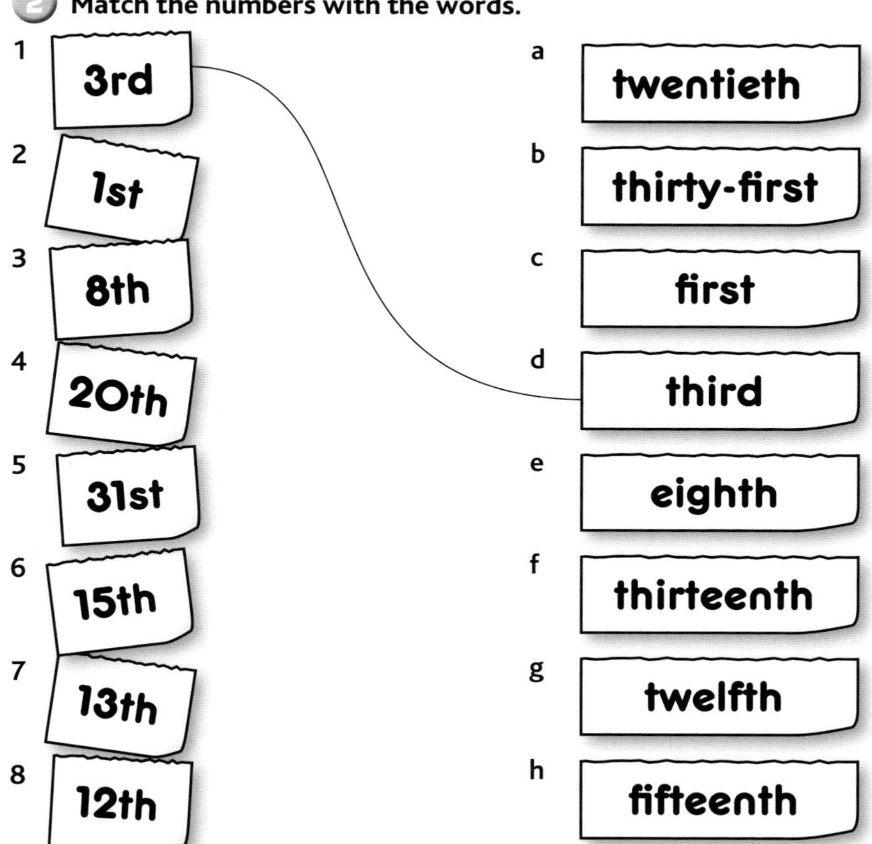


## Grammar: *like*; Object pronouns

**3 Choose the correct words.**

1 I *like* / *likes* pop music.
2 He *like* / *likes* basketball.
3 My brother *don't* / *doesn't* like History.
4 Joe *like* / *likes* Maths.
5 I *don't* / *doesn't* like oranges.
6 I *like* / *likes* strawberry cake.

**4 Match the questions with the answers.**

1 Do you like her?
2 Does she like you?
3 Does your brother like pop music?
4 Do you like PE?
5 Do you like films?
6 Does Sam like us?

a Yes I do. I like sports.
b Yes, I like them very much.
c Yes, he does. We're good friends.
d Yes, I do. She's nice.
e No, he doesn't. He likes rap!
f No, she doesn't. She likes my brother!

# B Activation exercises

## Vocabulary: Months; Ordinal numbers 1–31

**1 Write the months in the correct order.**

Dec Mar Jun Apr Sep Nov Jul Aug Feb Oct ~~Jan~~ May

1 *January*
2 ..........
3 ..........
4 ..........
5 ..........
6 ..........
7 ..........
8 ..........
9 ..........
10 ..........
11 ..........
12 ..........

**2 Write the numbers in words.**

1 11th *eleventh*
2 9th ..........
3 21st ..........
4 3rd ..........
5 12th ..........
6 2nd ..........
7 17th ..........
8 15th ..........

**3 Look at Terry's diary and complete the email.**

JULY

| | |
|---|---|
| **Monday 22nd**<br>[1] My birthday! | **Friday 26th**<br>[5] School finishes! |
| **Tuesday 23rd**<br>[2] Karate club tournament | **Saturday 27th**<br>[6] My brother's football match |
| **Wednesday 24th**<br>[3] My sister's birthday! | **Sunday 28th**<br>[7] Dad's barbecue |
| **Thursday 25th**<br>[4] Class party! | **Notes** |

JUL
Mo
Tue
We

Dear James,

We've got a busy week! Look at this!

1 It's *my birthday* on the *twenty-second of July*.
2 I've got a .......... on the ...........
3 It's .......... on the ...........
4 We've got a .......... on the ...........
5 .......... on the ...........
6 It's .......... on the ...........
7 It's .......... on the ...........

What have you got this week?

Terry

## Grammar: *like*; Object pronouns

**4 Choose the correct answers.**

1 Do you like cake?
  (a) Yes, I do. b Yes, he does.
2 Do you and your friend like apples?
  a No, we don't. b No, they don't.
3 Does your dad like his job?
  a Yes, he do. b Yes, he does.
4 Do teachers like books?
  a Yes, they do. b Yes, they does.
5 Does your sister like CDs?
  a No, he doesn't. b No, she doesn't.

## 5 Complete the table.

| + | - | ? |
|---|---|---|
| I like | I [1] *don't* like | [2] ......... I like? |
| You [3] ......... | You don't [4] ......... | Do [5] ......... like? |
| He / She [6] ......... | He / She [7] ......... like | [8] ......... he / she like? |
| We like | We don't like | Do we like? |
| They [9] ......... | [10] ......... | Do they like? |

## 6 Complete the sentences with the correct form of *like*.

1 (☹) I *don't like* oranges.

2 (?) ......... you ......... burgers?

3 (☺) They ......... pop music.

4 (☹) We ......... strawberry ice cream.

5 (?) ......... he ......... Spanish films?

6 (☺) I ......... English books.

7 (☺) She ......... her blue sofa.

8 (?) ......... he ......... computer games?

## 7 Complete the sentences. Use some words more than once.

her him it them us

1 (Sundays) Do you like *them*?
2 (pop music) I don't like .........
3 (my aunt) I visit ......... twice a week.
4 (your books) Have you got .........?
5 (Mark) I like ......... He's my friend.
6 (my homework) I do ......... five days a week.
7 (my friend and me) Come and see .........!
8 (my CDs) I've got ......... They're in my bag.

## 8 Complete Kiki's blog with the correct form of *like*.

Hi! I'm Kiki and this is my first blog. I'm twelve years old and I go to school in London. I've got two sisters, Maria (14) and Popi (9).
I [1] (☺) *like* pop music – my favourite singer is James Morrison and my favourite band is The Saturdays. They're so cool! But Popi [2] (☹) ......... them. She [3] (☺) ......... The Sugababes. Which bands and singers [4] (?) ......... you .........?
[5] (?) ......... you ......... the photo? These are my school friends Lottie and Mia. We [6] (☺) ......... PE. It's my favourite subject at school! I [7] (☺) ......... swimming and tennis. Lottie and Mia [8] (☺) ......... Science, too but I [9] (☹) ......... it. And you? [10] (?) ......... you ......... sports? What are your favourite subjects?
Bye for now!
Kiki

## 9 Write your blog. Use these ideas.

Write:

- how old you are.
- about you, your family and friends.
- about things you and your friends like.

.........................................................................

.........................................................................

.........................................................................

.........................................................................

.........................................................................

.........................................................................

.........................................................................

.........................................................................

.........................................................................

.........................................................................

.........................................................................

# B Extension exercises

## Vocabulary: Months; Ordinal numbers 1–31

**1 Complete the sentences with the months.**

1 My cousin's birthday is in ..............................
2 School starts in ..............................
3 My birthday's in ..............................
4 My friend's birthday is in ..............................
5 School finishes in ..............................
6 Football matches start in ..............................
7 There are thirty-one days in ..............................,
..............................., ...............................,
..............................., ...............................,
............................... and ...............................
8 There are thirty days in ..............................,
..............................., ...............................
and ..............................

**2 Write sentences about Class 2C.**

| SCIENCE TEST – CLASS 2C | | | | | |
|---|---|---|---|---|---|
| 1 | Annie | 100% | 9 | Petra | 75% |
| 2 | Josh | 96% | 10 | Sadie | 74% |
| 3 | Leela | 92% | 11 | Luka | 70% |
| 4 | Katie | 90% | 12 | Nigel | 69% |
| 5 | Simon | 88% | 13 | David | 67% |
| 6 | Harry | 85% | 14 | Peter | 64% |
| 7 | Joe | 82% | 15 | Grace | 62% |
| 8 | Fred | 80% | 16 | Ana | 56% |

1 (Josh) *Josh is second in the class.*
2 (Grace) ..............................
3 (Fred) ..............................
4 (Peter) ..............................
5 (Annie) ..............................
6 (Leela) ..............................
7 (David) ..............................
8 (Nigel) ..............................

Write two more sentences about other students.

9 ..............................
10 ..............................

## About you

**3 Write sentences with dates.**

three family birthdays

1 *My cousin's birthday is on 31st March.*
2 ..............................
3 ..............................

your next English lesson

4 ..............................

a friend's birthday party

5 ..............................

## Grammar: *like*; Object pronouns

**4 Look at the table and write sentences.**

| | cereal bars | ice cream | strawberries | burgers |
|---|---|---|---|---|
| Katya | ✗ | ✓ | ✓ | ✗ |
| Lucasz | ✗ | ✓ | ✓ | ✗ |
| Roberto | ✓ | ✗ | ✗ | ✓ |
| Adriana | ✓ | ✗ | ✗ | ✓ |

1 Katya *Katya likes ice cream and strawberries but she doesn't like cereal bars and burgers.*
2 Lucasz ..............................
3 Katya and Lucasz ..............................
4 Roberto ..............................
5 Adriana ..............................
6 Roberto and Adriana ..............................

**5 Look at the table in Exercise 4 and answer the questions.**

1 Does Katya like strawberries?
*Yes, she likes them.*
2 Do Katya and Lucasz like burgers?
..............................
3 Do Katya and Lucasz like ice cream?
..............................
4 Does Katya like cereal bars?
..............................
5 Do Roberto and Adriana like cereal bars?
..............................
6 Does Adriana like ice cream?
..............................

## Speaking: Give directions

**1 Complete the dialogues.**

It's near the supermarket, on the left.
Sorry, I don't know that road. Yes, we do.

1 A: Excuse me. Do you know this area?
B: ..........
2 A: Where's Green Park Road?
B: ..........
3 A: Where's the sports centre?
B: ..........

**2 Complete the dialogue.**

*Mario is from Brazil and he's in London.*

**Mario:** Excuse me.[1] Do you know this area?
**Jo and Tim:** Yes, [2] ..........
**Mario:** [3] .......... Brazilian Embassy?
**Jo:** Sorry, I [4] ..........
**Mario:** The address is 32 Green Street.
[5] .......... Green Street?
**Tim:** It's near Marble Arch Station.

## Writing: Write directions

**3 Read the email and look at the map. Where is the restaurant? Circle a, b or c. Then add commas to the email.**

Hi, Mel James and Nina!

The name of the restaurant for my party is 18. It's got sandwiches burgers cake and ice cream.

We haven't got the CDs and party hats – have you got any?

Here is a map and directions to the restaurant. It's near the station and there's a cinema a music shop and a newsagent's next to the restaurant. It's opposite the café – three buses stop there. The shops and the restaurant are on High Street.

See you on Friday!

Lewis

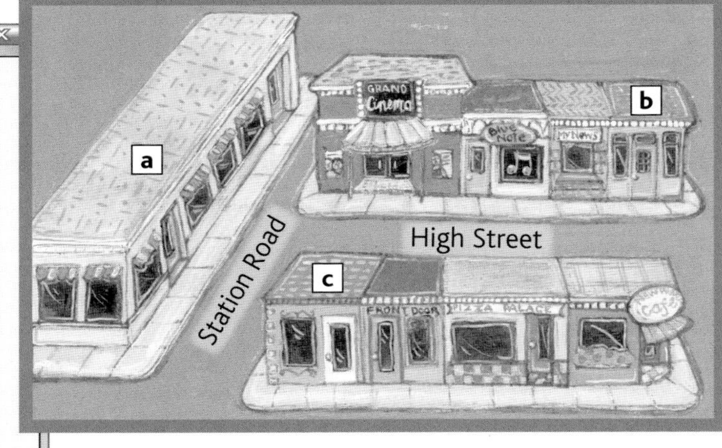


### Your turn

**4 Write directions to your school from your house. Then draw a map.**

..........
..........
..........
..........
..........
..........
..........
..........
..........

# Check

**1 Read and answer *True* (*T*) or *False* (*F*).**

## Class 2A survey results: Our favourite things

There are twenty students in our class.

| *The question:* | *Our answers:* |
|---|---|
| What's your favourite month? | Our favourite month is July. Second is December and August is third. |
| What's your favourite film? | *Harry Potter* is the favourite. *Lord of the Rings* is second and third is *Pirates of the Caribbean*. |
| Do you like ICT? | Fourteen students like ICT. Three say it's OK and three don't like it. |
| Do you like Lady Gaga? | Seventeen students like her and three don't like her. |
| What's your favourite type of music? | First is pop music, then rap and hip hop. |
| How often do you go to the sports centre? | Thirteen students go to the sports centre every week. Five students go twice a week and two go once a month. |
| How often do you play computer games? | Eleven students play computer games every day. Six students sometimes play them and three never play them. |
| What's your favourite computer game? | Our favourite game is *Saturday Games*. Second is *World Cup Football* and third is *Cool Dog*. |

1 August is the students' third favourite month. [T]
2 The students' second favourite film is *Harry Potter*. [ ]
3 Fourteen students don't like ICT. [ ]
4 Three students don't like Lady Gaga. [ ]
5 The students' favourite type of music is pop music. [ ]
6 Five students go to the sports centre twice a month. [ ]
7 Three students never play computer games. [ ]
8 The students' favourite computer game is *Cool Dog*. [ ]

**Score:** ........ **/7**

**2 Which word is different? Choose.**

1 book shop supermarket café (sixteen)
2 twelfth blog first twentieth
3 June November Green Road April
4 sports every twice once
5 swimming pool karate station music shop
6 second fifth third nine
7 me her like him
8 Sunday May March July
9 right left opposite email

**Score:** ........ **/8**

**Colour one ring on Lenny's tail for each correct answer.**

My score is ..................!

# 7 Holidays

## A Foundation exercises

### Vocabulary: Sports

**1 Write the sports words.**

| play basketball | ride a bike | rollerblade | skateboard | ~~ski~~ | swim |
|---|---|---|---|---|---|

1 ..........ski..........

2 ..............................

3 ..............................

4 ..............................

5 ..............................

6 ..............................

**2 Complete the sports words.**

1 r*u*n
2 sur.....
3 p.....ay volle.....ball
4 ri.....e a h.....rse
5 sa.....l a b.....at
6 s.....i

### Grammar: can

**3 Choose the correct words.**

1 (✓) I *can* / *can't* surf. (*can* circled)
2 (✓) He *can* / *can't* play basketball.
3 (✗) I *can* / *can't* ride a bike.
4 (✗) We *can* / *can't* ride a horse.
5 (✓) She *can* / *can't* swim.
6 (✓) They *can* / *can't* skateboard.
7 (✗) She *can* / *can't* sail a boat.
8 (✓) You *can* / *can't* rollerblade.

**4 Complete the dialogues with *can* or *can't*.**

1 **A:** ....*Can*.... you ride a horse?
**B:** Yes, I ....*can*.....
2 **A:** .................... you ride a bike?
**B:** Yes, I .....................
3 **A:** .................... you play volleyball?
**B:** No, I .....................
4 **A:** .................... you surf?
**B:** No, we .....................
5 **A:** .................... you skateboard?
**B:** Yes, we ....................!
6 **A:** .................... you ski?
**B:** No, I .....................
7 **A:** .................... you sail a boat?
**B:** No, we .....................
8 **A:** .................... you swim?
**B:** Yes, we .....................

# A Activation exercises

## Vocabulary: Sports

**1 Write the sports words and phrases. There are five extra words and phrases.**

| play basketball | play volleyball | ride a bike | ride a horse | | |
|---|---|---|---|---|---|
| ~~rollerblade~~ | sail a boat | skateboard | ski | surf | swim |

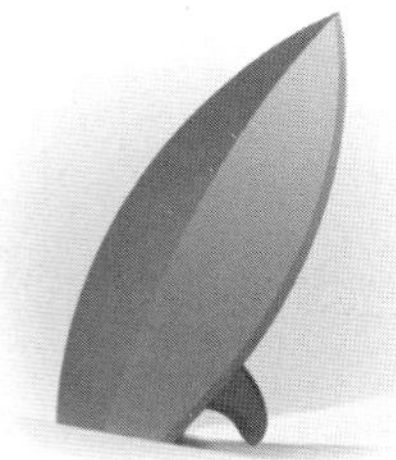

1 *rollerblade* 2 .................... 3 .................... 4 .................... 5 ....................

**2 Complete the sentences. Use words from the box in Exercise 1.**

1 Emma can't *ride* a horse.
2 I go to the swimming pool once a week. I can .................... 200 metres.
3 My brother can .................... a boat.
4 I .................... a bike to school.
5 Of course I can ....................! I love snow!

## Grammar: *can*

**3 Look at the table and answer the questions.**

| | swim | ride a bike | ride a horse | play volleyball | skateboard | surf | rollerblade | sail a boat |
|---|---|---|---|---|---|---|---|---|
| Maria | ✓ | ✗ | ✗ | ✓ | ✓ | ✗ | ✓ | ✓ |
| Peter | ✓ | ✓ | ✗ | ✓ | ✓ | ✗ | ✗ | ✗ |

1 Can Maria rollerblade? *Yes, she can.*
2 Can Peter sail a boat? ....................
3 Can Peter play volleyball? ....................
4 Can Maria ride a horse? ....................
5 Can Maria and Peter swim? ....................
6 Can Maria and Peter surf? ....................
7 Can Peter ride a bike? ....................
8 Can Maria ride a bike? ....................

**4 Look at the table in Exercise 3 and write questions and answers.**

1 Maria | swim?
*Can Maria swim?*
*Yes, she can.*

2 Maria and Peter | skateboard?
....................
....................

3 Maria | sail a boat?
....................
....................

4 Peter | ride a horse?
....................
....................

5 Peter | rollerblade?
....................
....................

6 Maria and Peter | surf?
....................
....................

## English today

**5 Complete the dialogue.**

| about me | doesn't matter | fact |
|---|---|---|
| ~~hopeless~~ | quite good | |

**Anna:** Come and join us at the swimming pool!

**Megan:** No. I can't swim. I'm 1 *hopeless* at it.

**Anna:** It 2 .................................. They teach you at the pool. And I can teach you, too. It's easy.

**Amy:** What 3 ..................................? I can swim! In 4 .................................., I'm 5 .................................. at it. I can teach her!

**Megan:** OK! Good idea, Amy!

**6 Complete the sentences with *can* or *can't*.**

1 I *can't* play volleyball. I'm hopeless at sports.
2 I .............. ride a horse. In fact, I'm quite good at it.
3 She .............. skateboard. She's the club champion!
4 We go on a skiing holiday every year, so we .............. ski.
5 That team isn't very good. They .............. play basketball!
6 Fred .............. surf but I can teach him. I'm very good at it.

## About you

**7 Answer the questions about you.**

1 Can you ride a BMX bike?
*Yes, I can./No, I can't.*
2 Can you play volleyball?
..................................................................
3 Can you and your friend ski?
..................................................................
4 Can your mother swim?
..................................................................
5 Can your best friend surf?
..................................................................
6 Can you skateboard?
..................................................................
7 Can your father sail a boat?
..................................................................
8 Can you ride a horse?
..................................................................

**8 Match the job adverts with the people. There is one extra person.**

1 ☐
Are you good at sports? Can you play basketball? Can you play volleyball? Come and work in our sports centre!

2 ☐
Can you swim? Can you surf? Can you sail a boat? Come and work with us at WaterWorld!

3 ☐
Can you ride a horse? A BMX bike? Can you rollerblade? Come and work with boys and girls from schools in the UK in July and August!

a

My name's May. I can ride a horse and I can ride a bike – I ride my bike every day. I can rollerblade, too. In fact, I'm quite good at it. I like school kids.

b
I'm Duane. I love water sports. I can swim, of course. I go to the swimming pool every day. I can surf and I can sail a boat, too.

c
My name's Sandeep. I can swim and I can ride a bike but I can't ride a horse. I'm quite good at football but I'm not very good at basketball. I can ski but I can't surf. I'm hopeless at it!

d
I'm Pippa. I love sports. Basketball and volleyball are my favourite. I'm in a volleyball team and I play three times a week. I'm quite good at it.

# A Extension exercises

## Vocabulary: Sports

**1 Match the words. Make five sports phrases.**

| | | |
|---|---|---|
| 1 | play | a boat |
| 2 | play | a bike |
| 3 | sail | horse |
| 4 | ride a | basketball |
| 5 | ride | volleyball |

1 *play basketball*
2 ……
3 ……
4 ……
5 ……

**2 The words are mixed up! Find and write six sports words.**

sk un · r im · su blade · rf skate · sw i · roller board

1 *ski* ……
2 ……
3 ……
4 ……
5 ……
6 ……

## Grammar: *can*

**3 Look at the questionnaire and answer the questions. Remember the commas in lists.**

**What can you do in English?**

| Can you: | Amy | Jim | You |
|---|---|---|---|
| 1 count from 1 to 100? | ✓ | ✓ | |
| 2 tell the time? | ✓ | ✗ | |
| 3 ask for personal information? | ✓ | ✓ | |
| 4 write about your favourite band? | ✗ | ✓ | |
| 5 talk about your house and your room? | ✗ | ✗ | |
| 6 describe people? | ✓ | ✗ | |
| 7 talk about routine activities? | ✓ | ✓ | |
| 8 write a party invitation? | ✗ | ✗ | |
| 9 talk about places in town? | ✗ | ✓ | |
| 10 talk about what you can and can't do? | ✓ | ✓ | |

1 What can Amy do?
*Amy can count from 1 to 100, tell the time,* ……
……

2 What can't she do?
*She can't write about her favourite band,* ……
……

3 What can Jim do?
……
……

4 What can't he do?
……
……

5 What can't Amy and Jim do?
*They* ……
……

### About you

**4 Complete the questionnaire in Exercise 3 about you. Then write two sentences about what you can and can't do.**

1 ……
2 ……

# B Foundation exercises

## Vocabulary: Parts of the body

**1** Choose the correct words.

**2** Complete the words.

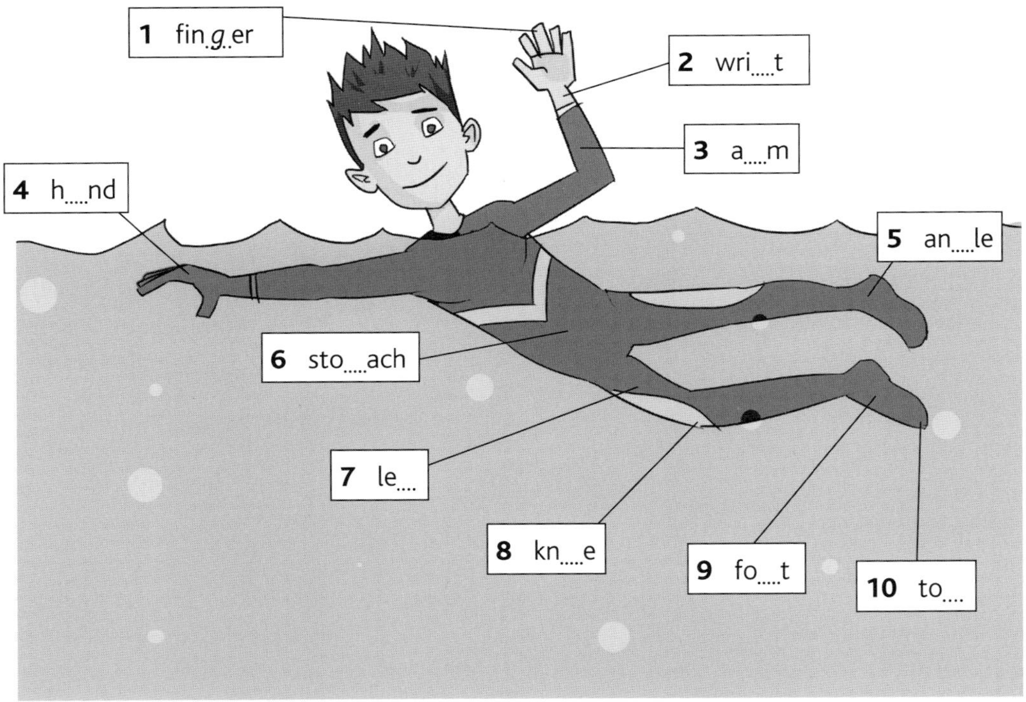


## Grammar: Giving instructions

**3** Match the sentence halves.

1 Stand — c
2 Move to
3 Don't
4 Don't stand
5 Touch
6 Do

a the left.
b near the TV.
c up.
d your nose.
e your homework.
f fall over.

**4** Write the instructions in the correct columns.

~~Stand up!~~ Don't move! Stop! Don't jump! Don't fall over! Move your feet!

| + | − |
|---|---|
| 1 *Stand up!* | 4 .................... |
| 2 .................... | 5 .................... |
| 3 .................... | 6 .................... |

# B Activation exercises

## Vocabulary: Parts of the body

**1 Write the parts of the body.**

| arm | ear | eye | finger | foot | hand | ~~head~~ | leg | mouth | neck | nose |
|---|---|---|---|---|---|---|---|---|---|---|

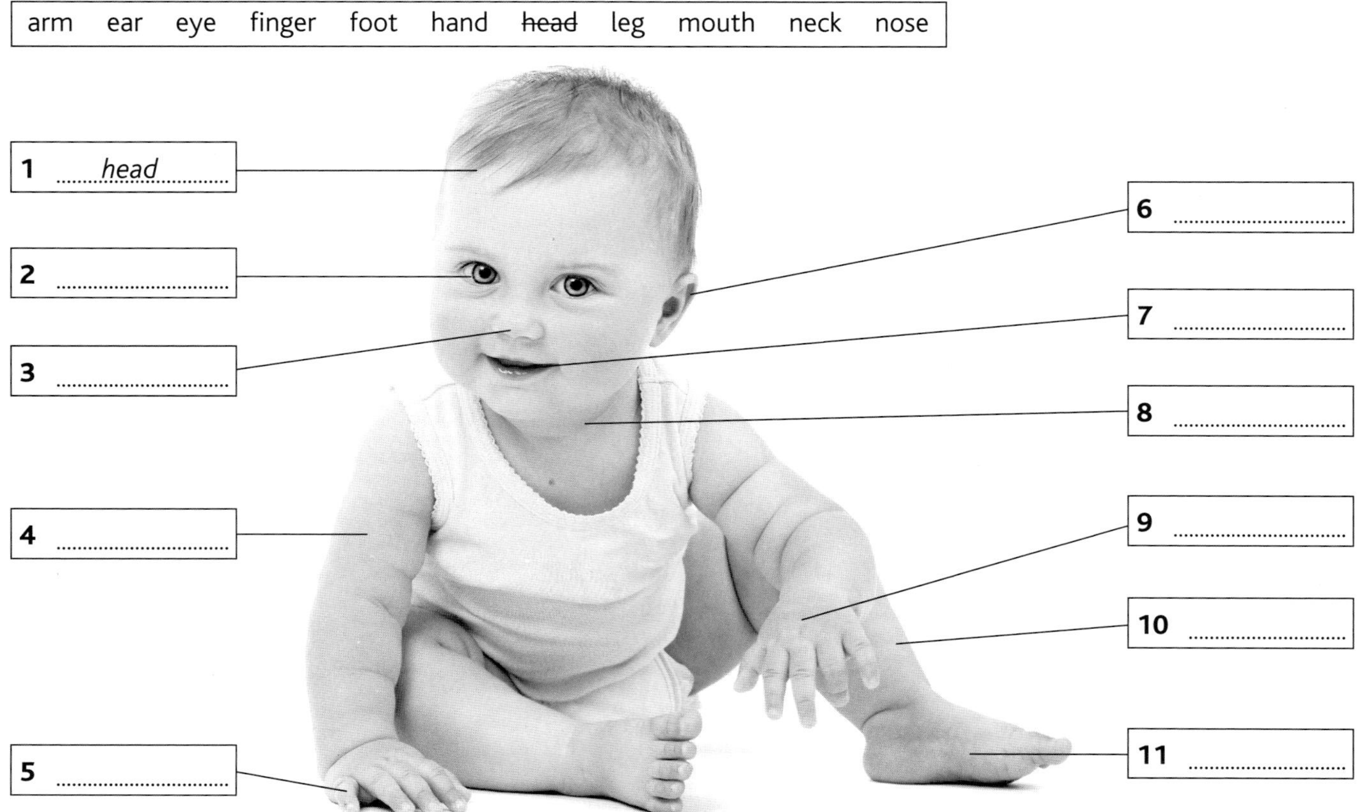


**2 Choose the correct words.**

1 You have ten (toes) / *fingers* / *ears* on your feet.
2 Your *neck* / *stomach* / *wrist* joins your hand to your arm.
3 My head is on my *leg* / *neck* / *ankle*.
4 I listen to music with my *neck* / *mouth* / *ears*.
5 Your *eyes* / *teeth* / *knees* are in your mouth.
6 Our *eyes* / *teeth* / *fingers* are on our hands.

## Grammar: Giving instructions

**3 Find the correct stickers.**

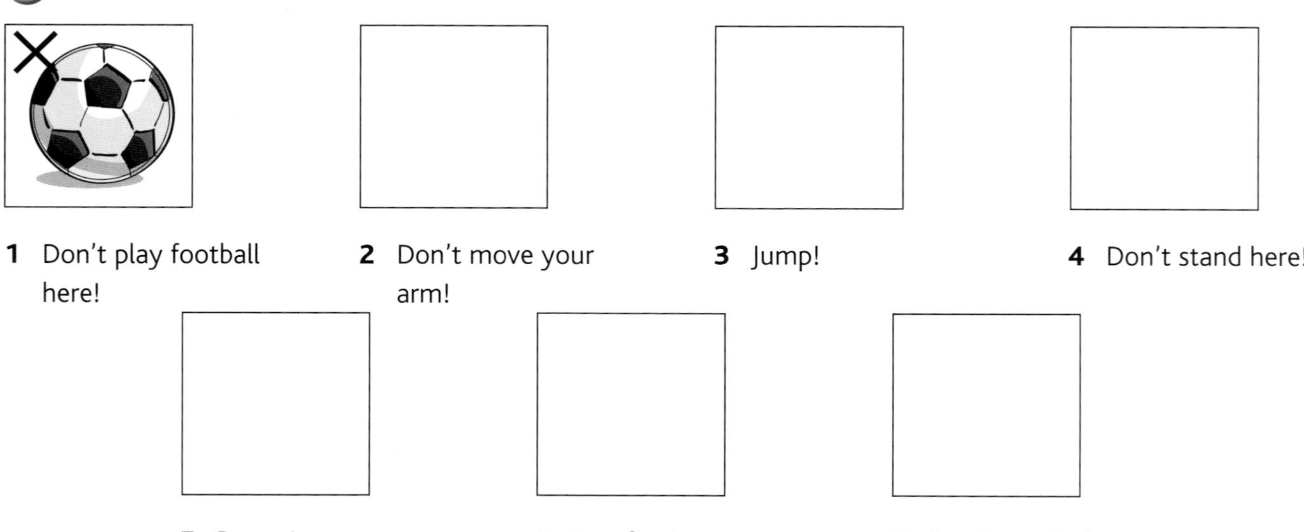

1 Don't play football here!
2 Don't move your arm!
3 Jump!
4 Don't stand here!
5 Dance!
6 Run fast!
7 Don't touch them!

## 4 Write the phrases.

| Don't talk. Jump to the left. ~~Jump to the right.~~ Listen. Move to the left. Move to the right. Don't write. |
|---|

1 *Jump to the right.*

2 ..............................

3 ..............................

4 ..............................

5 ..............................

6 ..............................

7 ..............................

## 5 Write the words in the correct order.

1 bathroom! guitar don't play in the your
*Don't play your guitar in the bathroom!* [H]

2 bed! on jump don't the
.............................................................. [ ]

3 to listen teacher your in class
.............................................................. [ ]

4 the ride don't bike your in house!
.............................................................. [ ]

5 every homework day your do
.............................................................. [ ]

6 your eat morning every breakfast
.............................................................. [ ]

7 don't on the in write the classroom! desk
.............................................................. [ ]

## 6 Are the instructions in Exercise 5 at home or at school? Write *H* (*Home*) or S (*School*) in the boxes.

## 7 Write the school instructions from Exercise 5 in the poster.

**SCHOOL RULES**

**In our English class:**

| ☺ | ☹ |
|---|---|
| • *Listen to your teacher in class.* | • .............................. |
| • .............................. | • .............................. |
| • .............................. | • .............................. |
| • .............................. | |

## 8 Make sentences and write them in the poster in Exercise 7.

1 go / to your lessons
2 talk / a lot / in class
3 speak / English / every day
4 talk / on your mobile phone / in class

## English today

## 9 Complete the dialogue.

| Can I have a go? I'm exhausted! That's it! |
|---|

**Anna:** Look, Megan, this is my new computer game, *Dance the Dance*. It's great!
**Megan:** Wow! [1] ..............................
**Anna:** Of course! OK, stand in front of the TV. Now jump to the left and move your arms.
**Megan:** Like this?
**Anna:** [2] .............................. You're good!
**Megan:** OK, your turn!
**Anna:** No, I can't play! [3] ..............................

# B Extension exercises

## Vocabulary: Parts of the body

**1 Write the parts of the body.**

**2 Which word is different? Choose.**

1 listen (basketball) ears music
2 hairdresser hair skateboard head
3 ankle guitar play fingers
4 trousers legs knees hat
5 sandwich eye mouth cheese
6 shirt shoes feet toes
7 nose eyes arm ears

## Grammar: Giving instructions

**3 Write the letters in the correct order to complete the instructions.**

1 (upmj) *Jump* twice!
2 (post) ..............................!
3 (ilsnte) .............................. to the music.
4 Move to the (flte) ..............................
5 (cutoh) .............................. your toes.
6 Move to the (grtih) ..............................

**4 Write the instructions from Exercise 3 under the pictures.**

1 *Listen to the music.*

2 ..............................

3 ..............................

4 ..............................

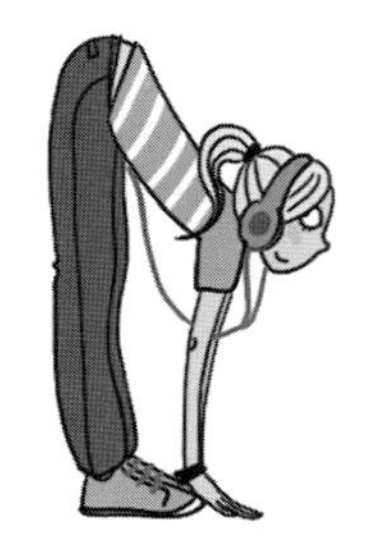

5 ..............................

6 ..............................

**5 What do you think? Read the ideas and write *Good* or *Bad*.**

1 Touch your toes every morning. *Good*
2 Play computer games forty times a week. ..............
3 Don't have breakfast! ..............
4 Run 500 metres every Saturday. ..............
5 Have an apple every day. ..............
6 Listen to your MP3 player in the History lesson. ..............

## About you

**6 Write four more good instructions for you and your friends.**

1 ..............................
2 ..............................
3 ..............................
4 ..............................

# C Foundation exercises 

## Vocabulary: Snacks; British money

**1 Complete the words.**

1 Melita has got some cri*s*ps, le.....onade and a bana.....a.
2 Simon has got some app.....e jui.....e, yo.....hurt and a ce.....eal b.....r.
3 Andy has got some bis.....uits, w.....ter and choc.....late.

**2 Write the prices in numbers.**

1 fifty pence ......*50p*......
2 ten pence ....................
3 one pound ....................
4 two pounds ....................
5 five pounds ....................
6 twenty pence ....................

## Grammar: Countable/Uncountable nouns

**3 Look at the picture in Exercise 1. Read and answer *True* (*T*) or *False* (*F*).**

1 Andy has got some biscuits. T
2 Simon hasn't got any bananas. ☐
3 Melita hasn't got any crisps. ☐
4 Simon hasn't got any apple juice. ☐
5 Andy hasn't got any yoghurt. ☐
6 Melita has got some water. ☐

**4 Choose the correct words.**

1 There are (some) / *any* apples in the bag.
2 There aren't *some* / *any* biscuits in the cupboard.
3 I want *some* / *any* water.
4 How much *is* / *are* the yoghurt?
5 Are there *some* / *any* bananas?
6 How much *is* / *are* the sandwiches?
7 We've got *some* / *any* snacks.
8 They've got *some* / *any* money.

# C Activation exercises

## Vocabulary: Snacks; British money

**1 Write the words in the correct columns. One word can go in two columns.**

| apple juice | ~~banana~~ | bar of chocolate | biscuits |
|---|---|---|---|
| cereal bar | crisps | lemonade | yoghurt | water |

| Food | Drink |
|---|---|
| *banana* | ............ |
| ............ | ............ |
| ............ | ............ |
| ............ | ............ |
| ............ | |
| ............ | |

**2**  **Listen and write the prices in the menu.**

### QUICK SNACKS

| SNACKS | PRICES |
|---|---|
| Crisps | 35p |
| Bar of chocolate | *£1.45* |
| Biscuits | 55p |
| Banana | 40p |
| Orange | ............ |
| Yoghurt | ............ |
| Sandwiches | ............ |
| **DRINKS** | |
| Apple juice | ............ |
| Water (bottle) | ............ |
| **SNACK COMBO** | |
| Sandwich + fruit + drink | ............ |

**3 Write the prices in words.**

1 20p *twenty pence*
2 £1.40 ............
3 10p ............
4 £5.50 ............
5 £2 ............
6 50p ............
7 £3.20 ............
8 45p ............

## Grammar: Countable/ Uncountable nouns

**4 Look at the menu in Exercise 2 and write sentences.**

1 there / crisps
*There are some crisps.*
2 there / cereal bars
............
3 there / apple juice
............
4 they / got / yoghurt
*They've got* ............
5 there / biscuits
............
6 they / got / lemonade
............
7 there / burgers
............
8 they / got / sandwiches
............

**5 Write questions about the snacks in Exercise 2.**

1 burgers? (they / got) *Have they got any burgers?*
2 lemonade? (there) *Is there any lemonade?*
3 biscuits? (there) ............
4 cola? (they / got) ............
5 water? (there) ............
6 bananas? (they / got) ............
7 chocolate? (they / got) ............
8 yoghurt? (there) ............

## 6 Match the pictures with the texts. There is one extra picture.

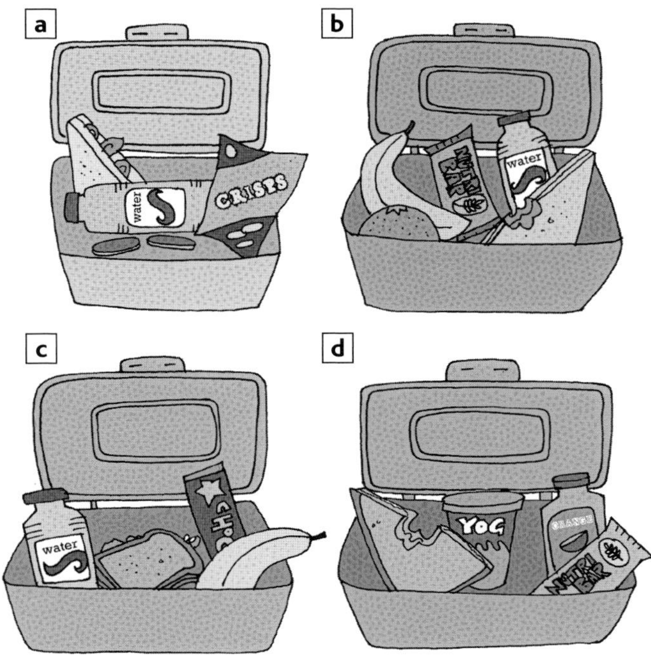


1 Will: I love biscuits but not in my lunch box. I usually have a banana and some water. I have a sandwich, too. I sometimes have some chocolate but I never have crisps. I don't like them. ......

2 Mark: I don't have any snacks in the morning. I always do sport in the afternoon, so I don't have a big lunch. I like a cereal bar and some yoghurt and a sandwich. My drink is usually orange juice. ......

3 Anna: I like chocolate biscuits but they're bad for you. For lunch I have a sandwich and some fruit – an orange and an apple or banana. I like cereal bars for a snack at eleven o'clock, too. I always have water with my lunch. ......

## 7 Look at Exercise 6 and complete the sentences.

1 In Will's box *there is some* ..........

..........

..........

2 In Mark's box ..........

..........

..........

3 In Anna's box ..........

..........

..........

## 8 Write questions and answers.

1 A: *How much are the oranges?*
B: *They're fifty pence.*

2 A: ..........
B: ..........

3 A: ..........
B: ..........

4 A: ..........
B: ..........

5 A: ..........
B: ..........

6 A: ..........
B: ..........

## English today

## 9 Complete the dialogue.

| idea | Relax! | the best | too | ~~up~~ |
|---|---|---|---|---|

**Kieran:** What's [1] *up*?
**Rosa:** I'm thirsty.
**Kieran:** Me [2] ..........! Why don't you get some fruit juice?
**Rosa:** Good [3] .........., but I've got my homework and it's late.
**Kieran:** [4] .......... It's OK! I've got some water in my bag.
**Rosa:** Oh thanks, Kieran! You're [5] ..........!

# C Extension exercises

## Vocabulary: Snacks; British money

**1 Find nine snack words.**

| J | B | D | I | R | F | X | M | B | S | C |
|---|---|---|---|---|---|---|---|---|---|---|
| E | A | P | P | L | E | J | U | I | C | E |
| H | R | B | V | F | W | D | T | S | K | R |
| Y | O | G | H | U | R | T | K | C | W | E |
| Q | F | H | E | M | P | G | V | U | E | A |
| A | C | R | I | S | P | S | D | I | G | L |
| K | H | E | A | Q | Z | C | P | T | O | B |
| E | O | K | D | W | S | R | U | S | F | A |
| F | C | L | G | X | B | Z | V | M | K | R |
| E | O | Z | D | B | A | X | Q | E | P | J |
| W | L | E | M | O | N | A | D | E | L | F |
| D | A | J | W | L | A | T | X | J | R | D |
| R | T | S | A | E | N | F | Y | E | I | E |
| D | E | G | F | W | A | T | E | R | R | O |

**2 Write sentences.**

1 10p + £1.30 = £1.40

*Ten pence and one pound thirty is one pound forty.*

2 75p + 45p = £1.20

..............................

3 £3.60 + £2.25 = £5.85

..............................

4 33p + 57p = 90p

..............................

5 35p + 89p = £1.24

..............................

6 £2.60 + £4.20 = £6.80

..............................

7 22p + 70p = 92p

..............................

8 £1.50 + 43p = £1.93

..............................

## Grammar: Countable/Uncountable nouns

**3 Complete the dialogue with *some*, *any*, *a* or *an*.**

**Jane:** Let's have [1] *a* snack. What do you want?

**Zack:** I want [2] .......... crisps and [3] .......... biscuits. Have you got [4] .......... chocolate biscuits?

**Jane:** No, we haven't. Why don't you have [5] .......... fruit? [6] .......... apple? [7] .......... banana?

**Zack:** I don't like fruit! I want [8] .......... apple juice, too.

**Jane:** There isn't [9] .......... apple juice. But there's [10] .......... lemonade and orange juice.

**Zack:** I don't like orange juice.

**Jane:** We've got [11] .......... yoghurt – do you like yoghurt?

**Zack:** Yes, I do! Give me [12] .......... yoghurt, please.

## About you

**4 Write your favourite snacks and their prices in the menu.**

Snack-a-snack

| Snacks | Prices |
|---|---|
| *apples* | *40p* |
| .......... | .......... |
| .......... | .......... |
| .......... | .......... |
| Drinks | |
| .......... | .......... |
| .......... | .......... |
| .......... | .......... |

**5 Write questions and answers about your menu from Exercise 4. Use *how much*.**

1 *How much are the apples?*

*They're forty pence.*

2 ..............................

..............................

3 ..............................

..............................

4 ..............................

..............................

5 ..............................

..............................

6 ..............................

..............................

7 ..............................

..............................

## Speaking: Buy a ticket for a sports event

**1 Complete the sentences.**

| have two tickets for today's match | much is that | the front, please |
|---|---|---|
| time does the match start | ~~would you like to sit~~ | |

1 Where *would you like to sit* ?
2 How ……… ?
3 Can I ……… ?
4 What ……… ?
5 At ……… .

### Your turn

**2 Complete the dialogue with the sentences from Exercise 1.**

A: Hello. [1] ………
B: Of course. [2] ………
Front or back?
A: [3] ………
B: Here are your tickets.
A: [4] ………
B: That's £9.50.
A: Here's the money.
[5] ………
B: It starts at quarter to five.
A: Thanks!
B: Enjoy the match!

## Writing: An advert for a sports fan club

**3 Complete the advert with *too* or *also*.**

**Share your sports DVDs!**

Have you got sports DVDs at home?
Bring them to our Share Club!
We [1] *also* want your sports magazines!

We meet in Room 36 every Friday at one o'clock and we watch football and NBA games on DVD. We sometimes read interesting articles from old magazines, [2] ………!

We [3] ……… have lunch in Room 36 – we have snacks. We usually bring drinks, [4] ……… .

Call Dave on 56780
or email shareclub@share-club.co.uk.

### Your turn

**4 Write an advert for your school's sports fan club. Use Exercise 3 and these words to help you.**

- have got / sports magazines, books and newspapers? bring / school sports fan club; also / DVDs and posters
- meet / Room 4 every Monday / four o'clock; read / talk about sports
- have snacks / Room 4; bring / fruit juice, too

………

# Check

**1** **Choose the correct answers to complete the text.**

***Meet Pete!*** He works in films and he [1] ....... do lots of things. He [2] ....... ride a bike. Look at the photo! He's very good at it! He can ride a horse, too. He can swim and he can also dance but he [3] ....... sing. He's hopeless at music! Here's Pete at work with film director Marty Scorcher.

**MS:** Pete, [4] ....... on the bike. Great!
**Pete:** OK!
**MS:** Now [5] ....... on your hands on the bike! Head in front, [6] ....... behind you.
**Pete:** Oh no, I can't do that!
**MS:** Yes, you can, Pete! I know you can!
**Pete:** OK, let's try. Oh yes, it's easy!
**MS:** Great, Pete! Brilliant! Now don't [7] .......!
**Pete:** Can I have lunch now, Marty?
**MS:** No, Pete. It isn't lunch time!
**Pete:** But Marty, I'm hungry! Can I have a snack? Look, my favourite: cheese sandwiches. Hey, how much [8] ....... the sandwiches?
**MS:** They're £1.75! OK, you can stop and have a sandwich.
**Pete:** Thanks, Marty! You're great!

**1** (a) can **b** can't
**2** **a** can **b** can't
**3** **a** can **b** can't
**4** **a** turn **b** jump
**5** **a** stand **b** surf
**6** **a** legs **b** nose
**7** **a** stand **b** move
**8** **a** is **b** are

**Score:** ....... **/7**

**2** **Write the words in the correct columns.**

~~knee~~ mouth pence pound run skateboard stomach water yoghurt

| Sports | Parts of the body | Snacks | British money |
|---|---|---|---|
| ........ | *knee* | ........ | ........ |
| ........ | ........ | ........ | ........ |
| | ........ | | |

**Score:** ....... **/8**

**Colour one ring on Lenny's tail for each correct answer.**

My score is ..................!

# 8 Time off

## A Foundation exercises

### Vocabulary: The weather

**1 Write the weather words.**

| cloudy | cold | foggy | hot | raining | snowing | ~~sunny~~ | windy |
|---|---|---|---|---|---|---|---|

1 It's ........*sunny*........ .

2 It's ............................ .

3 It's ............................ .

4 It's ............................ .

5 It's ............................ .

6 It's ............................ .

7 It's ............................ .

8 It's ............................ .

### Grammar: Present continuous

**2 Choose the correct words.**

1 I'm *swim* / *(swimming)* in the sea.
2 I'm *relaxing* / *relax* on the beach.
3 Look! It's *snow* / *snowing*!
4 He's *have* / *having* a great time.
5 We're *listening* / *listen* to music.
6 They're *playing* / *play* computer games.
7 It's *raining* / *rain* today.
8 She's *drink* / *drinking* lemonade.

**3 Complete the sentences with *am*, *is* or *are*.**

1 Will .......*is*....... talking to Mark.
2 Amy ..................... having dinner.
3 We ..................... doing our homework.
4 They ..................... playing volleyball.
5 I ..................... relaxing in my room.
6 Mark ..................... reading a book.
7 You ..................... writing an email.
8 Oh no! It ..................... raining.

# A Activation exercises

## Vocabulary: The weather

**1 Find the correct stickers.**

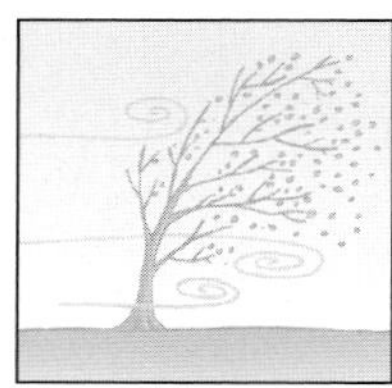
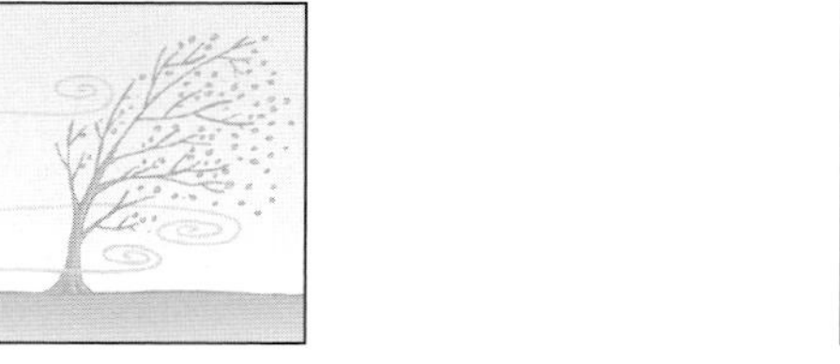

1 It's windy. 2 It's hot. 3 It's cloudy.

4 It's cold. 5 It's foggy. 6 It's sunny.

## Grammar: Present continuous

**2 Complete the table.**

~~am~~ are having making raining 're reading 's swimming

| | | | |
|---|---|---|---|
| I | 'm/[1] *am* | listening | to music. |
| You | 're/[2] ........ | [3] ........ | a book. |
| He/She | [4] ......../is | [5] ........ | in the pool. |
| It | 's/is | [6] ......... . | |
| We | 're/are | [7] ........ | fun. |
| They | [8] ......../are | [9] ........ | lunch. |

**3 Complete the table.**

| Verb | Verb + *-ing* |
|---|---|
| [1] play | *playing* |
| [2] rain | ........ |
| [3] have | ........ |
| [4] make | ........ |
| [5] swim | ........ |
| [6] wear | ........ |
| [7] sit | ........ |
| [8] drink | ........ |

**4 Complete the sentences.**

are having are playing are talking 's eating 'm sitting ~~'s talking~~ 's watching

1 Mark *'s talking* to Will.
2 Amy ........ her breakfast.
3 My friends ........ a great time.
4 My brothers ........ football.
5 I ........ in the living room.
6 Anna ........ TV.
7 My friend and I ........ on the phone.

## 5 Write the words in the correct order.

1 are | we | the | lunch | in | eating | kitchen

*We are eating lunch in the kitchen.*

2 watching | I | in | TV | living room | the | am

..........

3 doing | his | is | homework | Joe

..........

4 is | red | a | dress | Katie | wearing

..........

5 a | having | are | they | great | time

..........

6 listening | are | we | our | to | new | CD

..........

## 6 Complete the text. Use the present continuous.

It's a hot, sunny day on the beach. Helen and her brothers are on holiday. Helen [1] *is having* (have) a great time. She [2] .......... (sit) on a towel and she [3] .......... (read) a book. She [4] .......... (wear) a hat and a T-shirt and shorts. At the moment she [5] .......... (talk) on the phone to her friend Emily. Her brothers, Ed and Sam, [6] .......... (have) a good time, too. They [7] .......... (play) football. They [8] .......... (wear) shorts and T-shirts, too.

## 7 Imagine you are on holiday. Write a postcard to your grandmother.

Dear Gran,

I'm having a great time on holiday! I'm ..........

..........

## English today

## 8 Complete the dialogue.

| Hang | it lovely and sunny | rather |
|---|---|---|
| remember now | the weather like | |
| ~~where I am~~ | Lucky | |

**Kelly:** Hi, Tom! Guess [1] *where I am*!

**Tom:** I don't know. Where are you?

**Kelly:** In London! It's our school day out.

**Tom:** Oh yes, I [2] ........... What's [3] .......... in London? Is [4] ..........?

**Kelly:** Yes! The weather's brilliant! It's hot today.

**Tom:** [5] .......... you! It's raining here and it's cold and cloudy.

**Kelly:** Wow! There's George Clooney! He's here in London today! [6] .......... on, I'm sending you a photo of him!

**Tom:** George Clooney? I'd [7] .......... see Angelina Jolie!

# A Extension exercises

## Vocabulary: The weather

**1 What's the weather like? Write sentences.**

| City | Weather | City | Weather |
|---|---|---|---|
| 1 Rome | | 5 Madrid | |
| 2 Paris | | 6 Athens | |
| 3 London | | 7 Lisbon | |
| 4 Warsaw | | 8 Istanbul | |

1 *It's raining in Rome today.*
2 ..............................
3 ..............................
4 ..............................
5 ..............................
6 ..............................
7 ..............................
8 ..............................

### About you

**2 What's the weather like in your country today? Write three sentences.**

*In Barcelona it's sunny today.*

1 ..............................
2 ..............................
3 ..............................

## Grammar: Present continuous

**3 Write sentences. Use the present continuous.**

1 we / eat / breakfast / now
*We're eating breakfast now.*
2 I / ride / to school / on my bike / now
..............................
3 my best friend / have / a piano lesson / now
..............................
4 my sister / visit / our aunt / now
..............................
5 our parents / watch / TV / now
..............................

**4 Complete Freya's holiday diary. Use the present continuous.**

My holiday diary 13th August

**2.10 p.m.**

We're on holiday in Italy and we 1 *'re having* (have) a brilliant time! It's sunny and hot here. Today my sister and I 2 .............. (ride) our bikes on the beach. Mum 3 .............. (sleep) on the beach and my two brothers 4 .............. (swim).

**3.00 p.m.**

Now I 5 .............. (read) a newspaper. It says it 6 .............. (rain) in the UK. I'd rather be here! My brothers 7 .............. (play) football now.

**6.00 p.m.**

Today we 8 .............. (eat) our dinner in a restaurant. It's pizza. I love pizza! And we 9 .............. (have) Italian ice cream. Yum!

### About you

**5 What are your family and friends doing now? What are you doing now? Write sentences.**

1 (your grandmother) *My grandmother is sitting in the living room now.*
2 (your father and mother) ..............................
3 (your brother or sister) ..............................
4 (your best friend) ..............................
5 (your grandfather) ..............................
6 (your cousins) ..............................
7 (you) ..............................

## Vocabulary: Activities

**1 Complete the activities.**

| ~~listen~~ song text tidy walk write |
|---|

1 ......*listen*...... to the radio

2 send a .................... message

3 .................... the dog

4 .................... your room

5 sing a ....................

6 .................... an email

**2 Complete the activities.**

1 su*r*f the Inter...et
2 c...ok d...nner
3 m...ke a san...wich
4 d...aw a pi...ture

## Grammar: Present continuous

**3 Choose the correct words.**

1 I *'m not / aren't* making a sandwich.
2 She *isn't / aren't* listening to the radio.
3 We *isn't / aren't* cooking dinner now.
4 They *isn't / aren't* surfing the Internet.
5 I *'m not / isn't* writing an email.
6 He *isn't / aren't* drawing a picture.
7 You *isn't / aren't* tidying your room.
8 She *isn't / aren't* walking the dog today.

**4 Match the questions with the answers.**

1 What are you doing? ...*c*...
2 What's she doing? ......
3 What are your parents doing? ......
4 What are your friends doing? ......
5 What are you and your friend doing? ......
6 What's he doing? ......

a He's surfing the Internet.
b My friends are playing computer games.
c I'm doing my English homework.
d She's buying a snack.
e Mum is cooking dinner and Dad is watching TV.
f We're making a cake.

# B Activation exercises

## Vocabulary: Activities

**1 Complete the activities.**

| draw | listen to | make | send | sing | surf | tidy | walk | ~~write~~ |
|---|---|---|---|---|---|---|---|---|

1 *write* an email
2 .................... a song
3 .................... the radio
4 .................... a picture
5 .................... the dog
6 .................... a text message
7 .................... a sandwich
8 .................... the Internet
9 .................... your bedroom

## Grammar: Present continuous

  **Listen and tick (✓) the correct picture.**

1 ☐

2 ☐

3 ☐

**3 Write questions.**

1 You're making a sandwich.
*Are you making a sandwich?*
2 She's listening to her favourite band.
..........................................................
3 They're tidying their bedrooms.
..........................................................
4 He's surfing the Internet.
..........................................................
5 You're writing an email.
..........................................................
6 They're listening to the radio.
..........................................................
7 She's sending a text message.
..........................................................

**4 Answer the questions about you.**

1 Are you listening to the radio?
*Yes, I am. / No, I'm not.*
2 Are you sending a text message?
..........................................................
3 Are you listening to music?
..........................................................
4 Are your friends playing games?
..........................................................
5 Are you eating a sandwich?
..........................................................
6 Are you drinking water?
..........................................................
7 Are you talking to your friend?
..........................................................

**5 Complete the tables.**

| - | | |
|---|---|---|
| I [1] *'m* not | tidying | my room. |
| You [2] .......... | reading | a book. |
| He/She [3] .......... | [4] .................... (cook) | lunch. |
| We aren't | [5] .................... (listen) | to the radio. |
| They [6] .......... | walking | the dog. |

| ? | | |
|---|---|---|
| [7] .......... I | talking | to Lucy? |
| [8] .......... you | doing | your homework? |
| [9] .......... he/she | surfing | the Internet? |
| Are we | [10] .................... (have) | dinner? |
| Are they | [11] .................... (make) | a sandwich? |

**6 Correct the sentences about the picture.**

1 Mum's cooking lunch.

*She isn't cooking lunch. She's talking on the phone.*

2 Mum's wearing a white T-shirt.

..........................................................................

3 Suzie is writing a text message.

..........................................................................

4 Suzie and Harry are sitting at a desk.

..........................................................................

5 Harry is sending an email.

..........................................................................

Mum

Suzie

Harry

**7 Write questions and answers.**

1 Megan / draw a picture

A: *What's Megan doing?*

B: *She's drawing a picture.*

2 Mark / play a computer game

A: ..........................................................................

B: ..........................................................................

3 Amy / drink some orange juice

A: ..........................................................................

B: ..........................................................................

4 Will and Anna / listen to their new CD

A: ..........................................................................

B: ..........................................................................

5 Mark and Megan / surf the Internet

A: ..........................................................................

B: ..........................................................................

6 Will / read his English book

A: ..........................................................................

B: ..........................................................................

## English today

**8 Complete the dialogue.**

Here I go! Bad luck Time's up. ~~Are you ready?~~

**Mark:** Hi, Will! Come and see my new computer game. It's great!

**Will:** OK. What do I do?

**Mark:** You've got one minute. Copy the activities. There are twenty but start with ten. [1] *Are you ready?*

**Will:** Yes, OK. [2] ..................................

**Mark:** Come on, Will! Move! You can do it! OK, that's it. [3] ..................................

**Will:** Have I got ten points?

**Mark:** No, you've got two! [4] .................................., Will!

# B Extension exercises

## Vocabulary: Activities

**1 Read the text messages and write the phrases.**

| | | | |
|---|---|---|---|
| lstn 2 the rdio | snd a txt msg | wrt an eml | srf the Intrnt |
| 1 *listen to the radio* | 2 ........ | 3 ........ | 4 ........ |
| drw a pctr | mk a sndwch | tdy yr bdrm | wlk the dg |
| 5 ........ | 6 ........ | 7 ........ | 8 ........ |

### About you

**2 Answer the questions about you.**

1 Do you make sandwiches every day?

*Yes, I do. / No, I don't.*

2 Do you send text messages every day?

........

3 Do you write emails on your mobile phone?

........

4 How often do you surf the Internet?

........

5 Do you sometimes cook dinner?

........

6 Does your mum usually tidy your bedroom?

........

## Grammar: Present continuous

**3 Write questions and answers.**

1 she / draw / picture

A: *What's she doing?*

B: *She's drawing a picture.*

2 he / write / email

A: ........

B: ........

3 she / send / text message

A: ........

B: ........

4 they / make / sandwiches

A: ........

B: ........

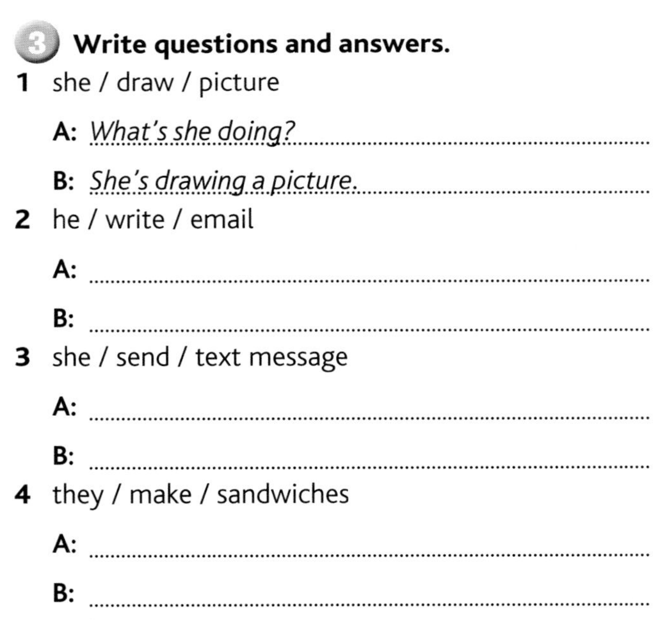

**4 Complete the dialogue. Use the present continuous.**

**Sadie:** Hi, Jake! Happy birthday!

**Jake:** Thanks! Guess what I [1] *'m doing* (do) today.

**Sadie:** [2] ........ (you / go) to school?

**Jake:** No, I [3] ........ (not go) to school. It's Saturday! Guess! There are lots of people here.

**Sadie:** Are you in town?

**Jake:** Yes, I am!

**Sadie:** [4] ........ (you / buy) presents?

**Jake:** No, I [5] ........ (not buy) presents.

**Sadie:** [6] ........ (you / stand) in the supermarket?

**Jake:** No, I [7] ........ (not stand) and I'm not in the supermarket. I'm in a book shop!

**Sadie:** [8] ........ (you / read) a book?

**Jake:** No, I [9] ........ (not read) a book. But I have got a book in my hands. It's a *Harry Potter* book.

**Sadie:** I don't know! What [10] ........ (you / do)?

**Jake:** I [11] ........ (meet) JK Rowling! She [12] ........ (come) to the book shop today!

**Sadie:** Brilliant! Can I come, too?

# C Communication

## Speaking: Make suggestions

**1 Match the sentence halves.**

1 I'm — c
2 Why don't we
3 What a
4 That's
5 Not
6 How about

a a good idea.
b a DVD again!
c bored!
d going swimming?
e pity.
f watch a DVD?

### Your turn

**2 Complete the dialogue.**

| a good idea | about going swimming |
|---|---|
| ~~I'm bored~~ | don't we watch a DVD |
| Not a DVD again! | What a pity. |

**Eddie:** Michael, [1] *I'm bored*.
**Michael:** Me too. Why [2] ..........? I've got some new ones.
**Eddie:** Oh no! [3] .......... I know! How [4] ..........?
**Michael:** That's [5] ..........! But ...
**Eddie:** But what?
**Michael:** It's Sunday today. The swimming pool is closed on Sundays.
**Eddie:** [6] .......... Hmm ... I know! Let's go bowling!
**Michael:** Yes! Brilliant! Come on, let's go!

## Writing: A postcard

**3 Complete the opening and closing phrases.**

1 H*i*, Jenny!
2 B...e!
3 De...r Mrs Smith,
4 Be...t wis...es,
5 Lo...s of l...ve,
6 Al... the ...est,
7 Y...urs,
8 Se... you soo...!

**4 Write the phrases from Exercise 3 in the correct columns.**

| Friends (informal) | Adults and people you don't know (formal) |
|---|---|
| *Hi, Jenny!* | .......... |
| .......... | .......... |
| .......... | .......... |
| .......... | .......... |

### Your turn

**5 Write opening and closing phrases for the postcards.**

[1] .........., Sophie!
We're having a great time in New York! I'm visiting lots of famous places and we're buying lots of presents for our friends.
[2] ..........!
Jodie

[3] .......... Aunt Jane,
We're having a great time in Greece. It's a brilliant place for a holiday. Today we're swimming and sitting on the beach.
[4] ..........,
Sam

# Check

**1** **Choose the correct answers to complete the texts.**

## Weather reports, January 31st

I'm in Manchester in the UK and [1] ..... snowing! It's cold and it's [2] ....., too. There aren't any cars but I can see some people. Let's ask this girl about the weather.

KEVIN: What [3] ..... you doing today?
GIRL: I'm [4] ..... my dog! But I'm going home now.

It's a bad day today. I'm Kevin Newton, UK News, Manchester.

I'm in Sydney in Australia and it's really hot and [5] ..... here! Right now I [6] ..... standing on the beach and people are swimming. Let's talk to this boy:

SHEILA: What are you doing today?
BOY: I'm [7] ..... a great time! I'm sitting on the beach and I'm talking to my friends. We [8] ..... eating lunch and listening to music.

Today is a good day in Australia. I'm Sheila Bruce, Australian News, Sydney.

**1** (**a**) it's **b** he's **c** they're
**2** **a** hot **b** cloudy **c** weather
**3** **a** is **b** am **c** are
**4** **a** walking **b** walk **c** walks
**5** **a** cold **b** snowing **c** sunny
**6** **a** 'm **b** 's **c** 're
**7** **a** has **b** have **c** having
**8** **a** 'm **b** 're **c** 's

**Score:** ........ **/7**

**2** **Write the words and phrases in the correct columns.**

~~it's sunny~~ tidy your bedroom write an email make a sandwich
it's foggy it's windy send a text message surf the Internet it's raining

| The weather | Activities |
|---|---|
| *it's sunny* | ........................ |
| ........................ | ........................ |
| ........................ | ........................ |
| ........................ | ........................ |
| | ........................ |

**Score:** ........ **/8**

**Colour one ring on Lenny's tail for each correct answer.**

My score is ..................!